contemporary
Bead & Wire
jewelry

contemporary
Bead & Wire
jewelry

Nathalie Mornu &
Suzanne J. E. Tourtillott

A Division of Sterling Publishing Co., Inc.
New York / London

Editors
Nathalie Mornu
Suzanne J. E. Tourtillott

Art Director
Stacey Budge

Photographer
Stewart O'Shields

Cover Designer
Barbara Zaretsky

Associate Art Director
Shannon Yokeley

Assistant Art Director
Bradley Norris

Art Interns
Nate Schulman
Emily Kepley

Editorial Assistance
Delores Gosnell

Editorial Interns
Kelly J. Johnson
Metta L. Pry
David Squires

Illustrator
Orrin Lundgren

Beaded Channel Ring,
page 93

The Library of Congress has cataloged the hardcover edition as follows:

Tourtillott, Suzanne J. E.
  Contemporary bead & wire jewelry / Suzanne J.E. Tourtillott and co-author
Nathalie Mornu.
      p. cm.
  Includes index.
  ISBN 1-57990-700-8 (hc)
  1. Beadwork. 2. Jewelry making. I. Mornu, Nathalie. II. Title. III.
Title: Contemporary bead and wire jewelry. .
TT860.T78 2006
745.594'2--dc22

                                    2005016774

10 9 8 7 6 5 4 3 2 1

Published by Lark Books, A Division of
Sterling Publishing Co., Inc.
387 Park Avenue South, New York, NY 10016

First Paperback Edition 2010
© 2006, Lark Books, A Division of Sterling Publishing Co., Inc.

Distributed in Canada by Sterling Publishing,
c/o Canadian Manda Group, 165 Dufferin Street
Toronto, Ontario, Canada M6K 3H6

Distributed in the United Kingdom by GMC Distribution Services,
Castle Place, 166 High Street, Lewes, East Sussex, England BN7 1XU

Distributed in Australia by Capricorn Link (Australia) Pty Ltd.,
P.O. Box 704, Windsor, NSW 2756 Australia

If you have questions or comments about this book, please contact:
Lark Books
67 Broadway
Asheville, NC 28801
(828) 253-0467

Manufactured in China

ISBN 13: 978-1-57990-700-6 (hardcover) 978-1-60059-590-5 (paperback)

For information about custom editions, special sales, premium and corporate purchases, please contact
Sterling Special Sales Department at 800-805-5489 or specialsales@sterlingpub.com.

For information about desk and examination copies available to college and university professors, requests
must be submitted to academic@larkbooks.com. Our complete policy can be found at www.larkbooks.com.

Contents

*Caught-in-Honey
Pendant, page 32*

Anemone Choker,
page 66

Introduction

The world has always had a love affair with beads. And who wouldn't fall for them? We're entranced by the abundance of color choices, their sparkle, and the way they feel as they trickle through your fingers.

A bead's "personality" is defined by its shape, material, translucency, and surface decoration. And for every kind of bead, whether faceted crystal, polymer clay, lustrous ceramic, or dainty seed, there's a beader somewhere who covets it. Vintage beads are prized by certain crafters; chunky, oversized beads made from resin or plastic are particularly of-the-moment. In a word, beads are fascinating.

Wire is the backbone of the jewelry shown in this book, and the projects demonstrate how truly versatile and beautiful it can be. The subtle gleam of metal, whether cool silver, glowing gold, or one of dozens of funky colored wires, gives every piece a polished look.

Just as there are beads and wires for every look and taste, the talented designers who share their designs in this book use a wildly wonderful range of styles, materials, and techniques. In fact, this collection represents some of the very best in bead and wire jewelry being made today. The necklaces, earrings, rings, and bracelets are so inventive and appealing that, seen together, we feel they elevate this type of jewelry to a new and exciting level. Now, more than ever, bead and wire is a jewelry technique worth exploring.

There are contemporary jewelry designs for every skill level. The remarkable Anemone Choker by Elizabeth Larsen practically reinvents bead and wire's traditional look. It might appear to be challenging to make, yet you may already be familiar with its main technique. Diane Guelzow's Wandering Gypsy Bracelet is eclectic, but its versatile style ensures a uniquely personal result every time. More experienced artists will find some intriguing wire techniques among the offerings. The delicate filigreed appearance of Rachel Dow's Temple Earrings gives new dimensionality to the extra-long style that's so popular right now.

Finally, the basics section has all the details about the supplies, tools, and tried-and-true techniques you'll need to make the projects in this book and create still more in your own designs. You can start with a few specialized tools and add what you need as you gain in aptitude and inspiration. Even the practice will be fun. So go ahead. Indulge your love for beads right now!

—Nathalie Mornu and Suzanne J. E. Tourtillott

Follies Chandeliers, page 81

Bead and Wire
BASICS

FOR AN ARTIST, it's no stretch to conceive of wire as a linear element, and beads as dots or points. The beauty of the projects in this book is that each transforms these simple building blocks into chic pieces to wear as ornament.

This chapter contains all the information you need to enter a world of creative expression making bead and wire jewelry.

Materials and Supplies

Shopping for the materials to create the projects in this book is a little like taking a trip around the globe: you'll find African trade beads, lampworked glass crafted in India, cloisonné treasures made in China, shimmering Austrian crystal, and wire from, well, all over.

Beads

If you've never worked in this medium before, you're in for some pleasant hours of bead browsing—the hardest part is stopping! You'll find a fabulous range of beads in glass, semiprecious stone, ceramic, and polymer clay; you can buy lampworked one-of-a-kinds, silver- and rhinestone-studded spheres, and cloudy moonstone orbs. Sift through bins of carved wooden beads; pick up some bits of dichroic or tumbled glass. Build a collection and store it in stacks of beaders' boxes with little compartments.

Most beads are organized in the stores by their material, shape, and diameter. (Tiny seed beads are sized using a special scale, in which the smallest ones have the highest numbers.) Be prepared to verify that your wire fits through your

You can keep your beads organized by storing them in small boxes with clear lids.

beads' holes: some very large beads can have surprisingly small holes, and vice versa. Unfortunately, there's no standard relationship between the size of a bead's hole and its diameter.

If you can't find beads to replicate the projects in this book, by all means purchase different styles; bear in mind that in doing so, you may achieve a completely different look, and you'll need to make certain that your selections match the bead sizes specified in the instructions.

BEADWISE

Wondering where to start when you look for beads? You could fill an entire dictionary with the evocative names of just the bead shapes that are available: rondelle, briolette, facet, montée, baroque drop, teardrop. What a whirlwind of choices!

Then there are the names that indicate a bead's function. A focal bead is one that stands out from all the rest, either due to its size or some other exceptional feature. Some have a strong, graphic quality; others use a carved or figurative motif. Spacers are generally smaller, plainer elements that are used to set off more exciting beads, but they too can be pretty interesting. Intricate little Bali beads typically come from the Indonesian island and are made from semioxidized silver; plainer-style heishi beads, originally made from seashells, are now available in stone and metals. Tube and bugle beads are long, slender cylinders, sometimes made of twisted metal. Finally, metal bead caps (and cones), placed at the ends of a round bead, can set it off and make it delightfully different.

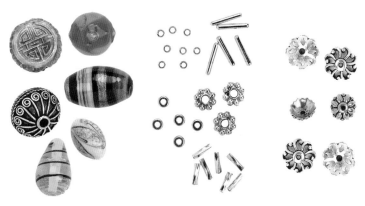

Focal beads

Clockwise from top left: spacers, tubes, Balis, twisted bugles, and heishi beads

Bead caps

*Square and round
wire profiles*

Wire

Traditionally, wire made from sterling silver or gold has been a popular choice for bead and wire jewelry, but many other wire products may be used too. Metal craft wire is now available in a wide variety of colors; relative newcomers include anodized and dyed metals such as aluminum, or niobium, which you can use alone or combined in the same piece of jewelry. Still other kinds of wire include brass, nickel, copper, and even platinum. Unlike these more malleable metals, super-springy *memory wire,* made from base metal or sometimes stainless steel, can be stretched and permanently bent, but it will always retain its initial coiled silhouette.

Whatever the metal, most wire comes in a large range of sizes and shapes, or *profiles.* Gauge is a scale of measurement that indicates a wire's diameter: the higher the numeral, the finer the wire. (Memory wire is the exception; it's sold in sizes to fit the neck, wrist, or finger.) Page 122 lists some helpful information

about wire gauges and their U.S. and U.K. specifications.

The projects in this book suggest that you use a specific size of wire, generally from 14 to 26 gauge. Using gauges other than those specified in the instructions is fine, but keep in mind that very thin wire, though easier to shape, isn't strong enough for a lot of heavy beads, and very thick wire isn't suitable for small-scale designs—not to mention the limitation of the size of a bead's hole. Wires of the same gauge will all feel a bit different to manipulate, because some metals are

softer than others. However, wire stiffens a bit as you work with it, adding more support to your work. This process is called *work hardening;* if wire gets handled too much, it becomes brittle and breaks.

Silver and gold wires are made and sold in different hardnesses: *dead soft*, *soft*, and *half hard.* In most cases, our designers have recommended the appropriate silver or gold wire hardness for their projects; when in doubt, use half-hard wire. Avoid dead-soft wire; it's difficult to work with and won't retain shaping or angles.

Many of the projects use sterling silver wire, but wire made from an *alloy* (a blend of less expensive metals) is an acceptable substitute, especially for jewelry for everyday wear or for working an unfamiliar design or technique. It's a great idea to use practice wire (of a similar gauge and hardness) if you plan to make a piece of jewelry from very expensive wire. Any inexpensive alloy wire will do.

Depending on the metal, wire is sold many different ways: on spools, in prepackaged coils, by

*Colored wire comes in a
range of hues and gauges.*

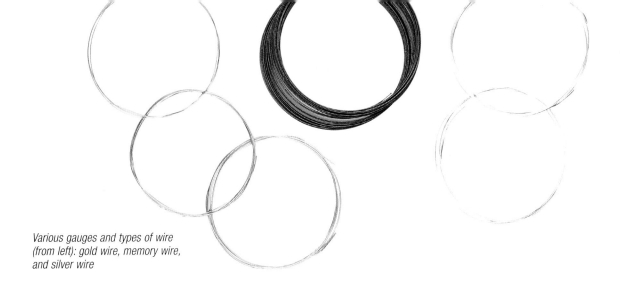

Various gauges and types of wire (from left): gold wire, memory wire, and silver wire

weight, and by length. Look for various types in jewelry supply shops, craft retailers, and in certain areas of hardware stores (including the electrical supply and framing departments). The Internet is also a vast resource for wire of every kind.

In addition to the plain round variety, wire is made with different cross-section profiles, such as square, half round, and triangular. Some wire companies sell lengths of pretwisted single-strand wire, or you can make your own with the pin vise tool, as explained later on. Twisted wire is also created when two lengths of nonround wire are twisted together for a beaded or rippled effect. Although most of the projects in this book are made with the common round variety, a few, such as the Beaded Channel Ring on page 93, use these novelty shapes, which create a completely different look. It's possible to alternate links of round, flat, and twisted wire with stunning results.

Festive Spiral Earrings, page 88

*Lantern Earrings,
page 100*

Clasps, Pins, and Such

Findings are prefabricated, basic jewelry pieces; they are made from many of the same kinds of metals that are available in unformed wire, and there are popular silver and gold options too. Necklaces may not need them, but bracelets almost always require clasps. To make an earring design wearable, use ear wires or posts; brooches sometimes need *pin backings*. Beads are often linked with *head pins* or *eye pins.* The head pin is simply a short, straight piece of wire with one flattened end to stop the bead, whereas an eye pin has an open loop at one end of the wire section. For either type, you form another loop at the other end after a bead has been strung onto it. Choose extra-long pins if you plan to add more than one bead.

It's easy to trim off excess wire, but there's nothing to be done when there's not enough. Just like wire, head pins and eye pins are available in different gauges. Be sure they'll fit through the beads' holes.

You can use commercial clasps or closures on any of the projects in this book, but in some cases our designers give you instructions on how to fashion them yourself, such as in the Sassy Pin on page 43. Making your own closures gives a piece of jewelry a more integrated look. Findings often become important elements to the overall design, so you'll want to take care that even purchased ones are made of materials of a quality and style that complement it.

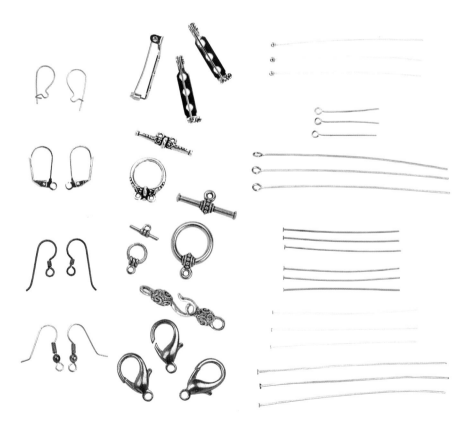

Left column: ear wires; center column (from top): pin backings, toggles, clasps; right column (from top): ball-end pins, eye pins, head pins

Jump rings are another popular finding. These simple rings, usually made from plain silver or gold, or from base metal, are great for connecting links. They can be found in a variety of sizes (by diameter and by wire gauge), or you can make your own (see the Handmade Jump Rings sidebar on page 19).

For the bead-and-wire jeweler, a commercially made chain can be a foundation to which beads are attached with head pins, or else with jump rings. You can buy various styles of chain—from very delicate to quite chunky—prepackaged. Some beading shops stock commercial chain on large spools and will cut it to the length you specify. In any case, for certain projects you might need to be able to open the chain's links. If the links have been soldered closed, you'll have to use jump rings or bead loops to attach anything to them.

Lucky Necklace, page 59

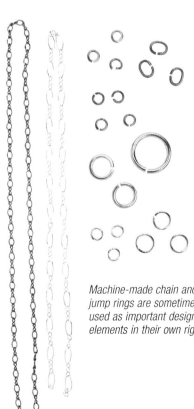

Machine-made chain and jump rings are sometimes used as important design elements in their own right.

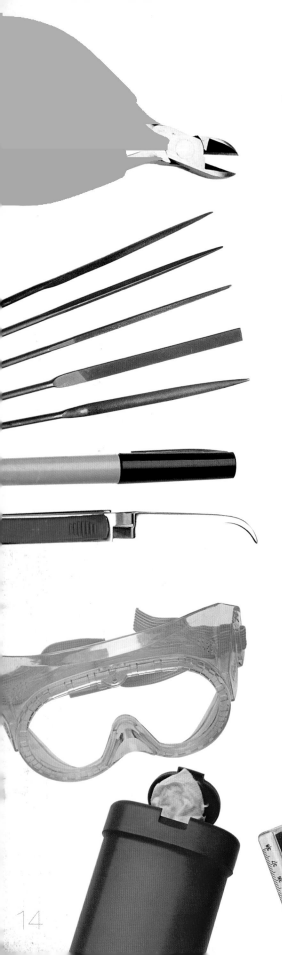

The Basic Tool Kit

In your tool kit you should have certain items that are indispensable for creating the jewelry in this book: wire cutters, needle files, pliers, crosslocking tweezers, protective eyewear, a pin vise or clamp, a permanent marker, and a ruler with both U.S. and metric measurements. Jewelry wipes, which are soft papers impregnated with polish, keep your work bright and clean. Each project's instructions presume that you have this basic tool kit, so only specialized tools needed to make a project are listed.

Wire Cutters

A good pair of wire cutters is essential for making all of the jewelry in this book. There are several different styles, but whichever ones you use, make sure they cut absolutely flush, since the shape of the cut's end, or *burr,* will need to be filed. The smaller the burr, the less filing will be needed. Since you will often need to cut wire in very small spaces, bigger is definitely not better. Pointed tips give you the most control.

Needle Files

Use a metal file with a fine tooth to smooth out the rough edges of cut wire ends and any other marring that may occur during the forming stages. Unfiled ends scratch and catch on fabric, so resist the temptation to ignore this crucial step. (And remember, too, that good wire cutters help ensure that you won't have to do a lot of filing.) Follow these rules: softer wire need be filed only with the finest of your files; start with a slightly coarser file for harder wire.

Pliers

Pliers are a bead and wire jewelry maker's best friend. Round-nose, chain-nose, and flat-nose pliers are the most-used types, although other, more specialized pliers can be found. To prevent damage to your wire as you work, select a type with smooth jaws rather than serrated ones. Inexpensive pliers are fine for beginners. If wire jewelry ever becomes your life's passion, you can easily trade up to a better brand.

Round-nose pliers are essential for making loops (described on pages 20–21). Because the jaws are wide at the base and tapered at the tip, you can vary the size of your loops depending on where along the jaw you place the wire to start.

The basic tool kit contains (from top): wire cutters, a set of needle files, a permanent marker, crosslocking tweezers, protective eyewear, jewelry wipes, and a ruler.

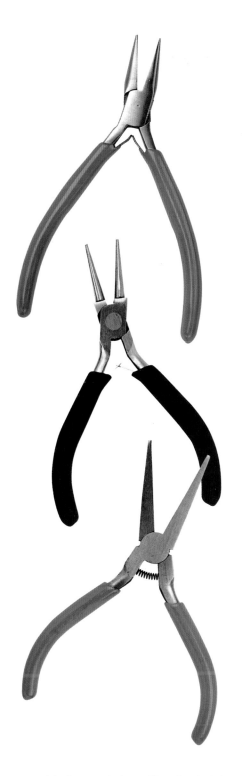

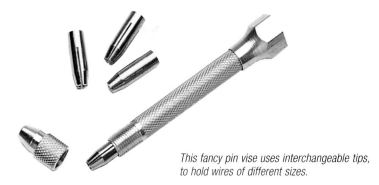

This fancy pin vise uses interchangeable tips, to hold wires of different sizes.

Chain-nose pliers get this name because they're ideal for opening and closing chain links. They're also useful for opening and closing loops and jump rings, working in tight spots, and, if you don't have special crimping pliers (read more about them in the Additional Tools section, on page 16), for crimping the ends of wire wraps. Chain-nose pliers are sometimes confused with needle-nose pliers, the electrician's tool that has serrated teeth in its jaws (though these can be used to add texture to wire). Flat-nose pliers resemble chain-nose pliers, but their jaws, instead of tapering, remain wide all the way to the tips. They're perfect for making sharp bends and for holding wire. Here's a tip: when working with colored wire, always wrap your pliers' tips with plastic tape to prevent marring the colored finish. For extra-gentle wire handling, you can sometimes find pliers with plastic-coated jaws.

Pin Vise

This simple tool allows you to create lengths of twisted wire in just minutes. You can work with a pair of pin vises, or use just one pin vise and some sort of clamp (or use pliers instead, if you have only a short quantity of wire to twist). See page 21 for an explanation of the technique.

A basic array of wire-working pliers includes (from top): chain nose, round nose, and flat nose.

Quatrefoil Earrings, page 71

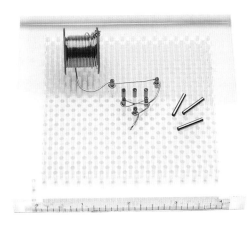

The tools shown on these two pages are used for only some of the projects; left, a wire jig; below, a ring mandrel

Tool Kit Additions

These tools, while not essential for every jewelry project, will be needed for some. Check the projects' tool lists before you begin.

Jig

A wire jig is a lifesaver when you're making a piece that uses multiple links made in the same shape, although lots of wire jewelry can be made without ever using one. Essentially, the tool is a base with a grid of holes that hold tiny, moveable pegs, around which you wrap the wire. The result: near-perfect consistency for each link.

Jigs are also a good design tool; just play around with some inexpensive wire and different peg placements to create your own wire patterns. Your local jewelry shop probably has books that contain a nice variety of jig patterns. You can purchase commercial jigs in craft stores or make your own with a block of wood and some finishing nails.

Mandrel

A mandrel is any straight or tapered rod around which you can wrap wire to shape it into coils. It's an essential tool for making jump rings, the loops in closures, or uniformly sized units for links. Metal knitting needles make ideal mandrels, but you can use a nail, a dowel, one of the metal rods of various diameters sold in hobby shops, or even a pen. Mandrels don't have to be round. For jewelry with a completely different look, try using a square, oval, or rectangular mandrel. For certain applications—for instance, when making long coils for jump rings— you might even try a coiling tool, but it isn't necessary for any of the projects in this book.

Hypnosis Ring, page 50

Hammers and Anvil

A few of the projects were hammered, or *forged,* to change the shape of the wire a bit. You can employ a common carpentry hammer and work on a smooth, very hard surface, such as a steel block or an anvil. To shape or flatten wire without marring it or changing the wire's profile in any way, use a rawhide or plastic hammer.

Crimping Pliers

A few projects use crimping beads, which are tiny tubelike beads made of metal soft enough to allow them to be compressed against wire or cord with a pair of crimping pliers.

Eggbeater Drill

This tool will enable you to rapidly coil long quantities of wire around a small mandrel and is particularly helpful for making a lot of jump rings. See the Handmade Jump Rings sidebar on page 19 to learn about using an eggbeater drill.

More specialty tools (from top left): steel block, anvil, rawhide and chasing hammers, eggbeater drill, and crimping pliers

17

Vortex Necklace, page 54

Wire Techniques

Now for the fun: learning how to wrangle the wire into a great jewelry design using basic wire techniques. Unless you're already familiar with them, you'll probably want to practice these techniques with a low-cost wire first—it's not easy to straighten wire once it's bent the wrong way. You might want to use the fun colored-wire products to make your learning curve more enjoyable. The results might be good enough to use for a later project.

Sometimes it may seem as if your wire has a mind of its own. To keep spooled wire under control, put it in a small plastic storage bag. Pull out a length of wire as needed. If you're working with a coil of wire rather than a spool, wrap a piece of masking tape around it so it can't spring open in all directions. Good-looking jewelry pieces are those with smooth and confident swoops, angles, and curves, made from kink-free wire.

Straightening

To keep it in good condition, wire is stored and sold in coils. Coiling wire saves space, but it's best to straighten out its curve before you begin working with it. To straighten a short length of wire, hold one end of it with chain-nose pliers. Just above the pliers, grasp the wire with a cloth or paper towel to keep your hands clean and to prevent friction burn. Squeezing your fingers slightly, pull the length of wire through them.

If the wire bends or crimps at any time, gently run your finger along it to smooth the kink, or rub the wire over the edge of a table padded with newspaper. Don't smooth a crimp too vigorously, or the wire could break. (Shaping wire, remember, hardens it. The more it's worked, the more brittle it becomes.)

Wrapping

No matter what you're wrapping the wire around, always pull it tightly against the pliers, mandrel, bead, or wire. When you're making jump rings, keep each pass of the wire as even and as close to the last one as possible.

Using Jump Rings

Always open and close jump rings by holding each end with pliers and twisting one ring's end toward you and the other end away, as shown in figure 1; pulling the ends straight apart, laterally, will distort the ring's shape and can undermine the strength of the wire and cause it to break.

FIGURE 1

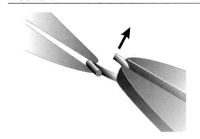

To make your own jump rings, simply wind a length of wire tightly around a mandrel. If you want to make a lot of jump rings at once, you might consider using an eggbeater drill to quickly do the job. Secure both the mandrel and one end of the wire tightly in the tool's jaws. As you turn the handle, hold the wire close to the mandrel. Whether you use a drill or not, keep the rounds of wire as straight and as close to each other as possible. After you've wound all the wire, slide the coil you've just formed off the mandrel and trim the ends. Use wire cutters, in exactly the same position each time, to free a fully circular ring—no more, no less—from the coil. One last tip: it's tempting to use your fingers to pry open a jump ring, but avoid splitting your nails by using two pairs of flat-nose pliers instead.

Spirals

To create flat spirals, use the tip of a pair of round-nose pliers to curve one end of the wire into a half-circle or hook shape about ⅛ inch (0.3 cm) in diameter (see figure 2). Use the very tips of the pliers to curve the end of the wire tightly into itself, as shown in figure 3, aiming to keep the shape round rather than oval. Hold the spiral in flat- or chain-nose pliers and push the loose end of the wire against the already-coiled form (see figure 4); as you continue, reposition the wire in the pliers as needed.

FIGURE **2**

FIGURE **3**

FIGURE **4**

Jellyroll Bracelet, page 120

*Venetian Reverie
Necklace, page 108*

Links and Loops

A link is simply one unit in a piece of jewelry. A link can be formed either by hand or with a jig. It can be an elaborate wire shape full of curls and curlicues or be based on a simple form, such as an S shape or a figure eight.

A *loop* is an important part of a link. The perfect loop should be precisely circular, centered over the straight part of the wire from which it's formed, and it should close tightly. Perfect your technique by making loops from different gauges of scrap wire.

Start with 6 inches (15.2 cm) of wire and work with a pair of round-nose pliers. Make a sharp 90-degree bend about ½ inch (1.3 cm) from one end of the wire, as shown in figure 5. This measurement will vary, depending on how large a loop you want to make; with practice, you'll get to know how much wire to allow for it.

Hold the wire so that the longer portion points to the floor and the short, bent end is pointing at you. Grasp the short end with the round-nose pliers, holding the pliers so that the back of your hand faces you. The closer to the tips you work, the smaller the loops you can make. Keeping

the tips themselves stationary, rotate the pliers up and away from you (see figure 6). Be careful not to pull out the right-angle bend you made earlier. Stop rotating when you've made half the loop.

Slide the pliers' tips back along the wire a bit and resume the rotation. To prevent the loop from becoming misshapen, make sure to keep one of the pliers' tips snugly inside the loop as you make it, so that the loop is being formed by a combination of rotation and shaping around the "mandrel" of the pliers. Keep working, sliding the pliers back as needed, until the loop is closed against the 90-degree bend (see figure 7). To make all your loops look nice and consistent, see the Same-Sized Loops (Every Time!) sidebar on page 21.

A *bead loop link* is made by enclosing a bead between two loops. Another option is to start with an eye pin, so that you'll have to fashion only one closing loop.

Of course, there are hundreds of variations of these basic links. Links can be attached to each other with jump rings or linked directly together as you make them.

FIGURE 5

FIGURE 6

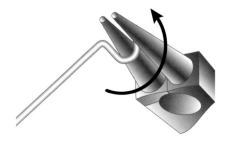

FIGURE 7

Sante Fe Cuff, page 41

A *wrapped bead loop* is a simple variation of the bead loop link just described. Use an extra length of wire for the 90-degree bend. Once you've made the loop, reposition the pliers so that the lower jaw is inside it. Use your other hand to wrap the wire's tail around the base of the loop several times, as shown in figure 8. Slide on one or more beads and, if the design calls for it, repeat the loop-forming process at the other end to make a *wrapped bead loop link* (see figure 9). Trim off any excess wire.

FIGURE 8

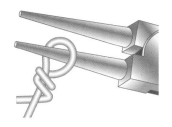

FIGURE 9

SAME-SIZED LOOPS (EVERY TIME!)

With a permanent marker, draw a line on the jaw of your round-nose pliers. If you place the wire there every time you make a loop, you can count on it always to be the same size.

A *wrapped bead loop* is a simple variation of the bead loop link just described. Use an extra length of wire for the 90-degree bend. Once you've made the loop, reposition the pliers so that the lower jaw is inside it. Use your other hand to wrap the wire's tail around the base of the loop several times, as shown in figure 8. Slide on one or more beads and, if the design calls for it, repeat the loop-forming process at the other end to make a *wrapped bead loop link* (see figure 9). Trim off any excess wire.

Opening and Closing Loops

Just as with jump rings, use two pair of pliers to open and close loops. Twist the cut end sideways while keeping the other side of the loop stationary. Pulling it open any other way will distort the loop's shape. Be sure to tighten any gaps in loops after you've attached your links.

Twisting

Only square wire can be twisted. Round wire won't show the twisting properly, and the process will just work-harden it.

To create twisted wire in no time at all, work with a pair of pin vises. Insert each end of a piece of wire into a pin vise, tighten the chucks, and twist them in opposite directions until you like the look you've achieved. If you have only one pin vise, secure the other end of the wire in a clamp or table vise (or in a pair of pliers if you have just a short quantity to twist). You can also use this tool to twist two lengths of the same wire together, creating a heavier look, or to twist together two different colors of wire.

Arabesque Necklace and Earrings, page 73

Jig-Formed Links

A jig tool helps you make the same wire shape (usually a link) consistently, over and over. To keep your links identical, always follow the same circuit on the jig and try to work in the same manner each time. Using flat-nose pliers, hold a piece of wire tightly at one end, or place its tail in an empty hole in the jig that's near the first peg (or nail). Wrap the wire tightly around the pegs, following the pattern indicated in the instructions. Once you've made one unit, remove it from the jig and repeat to make all the units that you need. It's that easy.

Polishing

You can polish your jewelry with a jewelry buffing cloth (sometimes called a *rouge cloth*) or papers, which are available from most jewelry suppliers. Before using any cleaning solution, test it on a scrap piece of wire first. A tumbler is an option for some pieces, but make sure you're familiar with its operation and consider that many beads aren't suitable for the process.

The Needle Arts

Crocheting and knitting with wire aren't all that different from the yarn variety—and you needn't worry about your project shrinking in the wash later. Because wire is thinner and more slippery than yarn, the techniques may feel a little awkward at first. Even if you already have experience, you'll find that when using wire, you'll need to use a light hand in establishing the tension (i.e., how tightly or loosely the material is woven together), because this material has no elasticity whatsoever.

Creating a slipknot requires a different approach than with yarn, since wire doesn't actually slip. Instead of pulling on one end to tighten it, tug on both. The wire loop should still be able to move easily up and down the needle or hook. As you work, resist the temptation to wrap the wire around your finger, as is typical when working with yarn, because it will create even more kinks and crimps. And although you can smooth the kinks somewhat, don't worry too much about them, because for the most part they won't be noticeable in the finished piece.

Often, all the beads in a project are threaded onto the wire before you cast

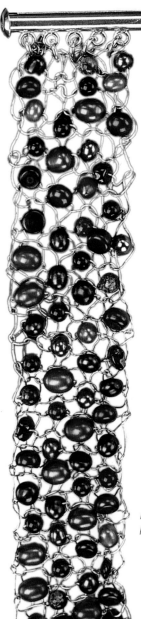

Mardi Gras Bracelet, page 46

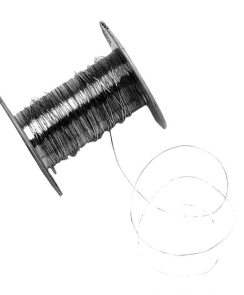

on, and then each one slipped into place as needed (usually after each stitch). As you cast on, be prepared to leave a tail long enough to finish the piece and hold the clasp.

Colored craft wire is popular for knitting and crocheting. If you'd like to try working with silver wire, consider using gold or *fine* silver wire, which is softer and lighter (though more expensive) than sterling.

Knitting

The projects in this book use only the knit or purl stitches, and they employ the standard knitting abbreviations you're used to seeing for yarn projects. Pull your knitting down and away from the needle as you go, flattening it slightly with your fingers, so as to make it easier to work the next row. Knitting needles come in different diameters and materials. Aluminum needles are more practical than wood or bamboo, simply because the wire will slip better on them, but what's most important is to use the size listed in the instructions in order to reproduce the project closely. Short, double-pointed needles are sometimes recommended for smaller-size pieces.

Crocheting

Crochet hooks also come in different sizes and may be aluminum, wood, or plastic; you can use a hook made from any material you like. Hook size affects how tightly or loosely woven the fabric appears between stitches, so if you want to duplicate the project, make sure to use the size specified in the instructions.

The only two crochet stitches used to create the projects in this book are the simplest ones—chain stitch and single crochet. Crocheted chain has a tendency to twist, so be prepared to do some smoothing as you work. Hold the loop you're working on with the thumb and finger of your nondominant hand so you can control its size and shape.

Time for lots of beady, loopy fun! You have a basic tool kit, some wire, and an exciting array of handpicked beads; you've practiced the techniques and know a wrapped loop from a bead link. You're ready for the rewarding handicraft of making bead and wire jewelry, and we have 43 delightful projects waiting.

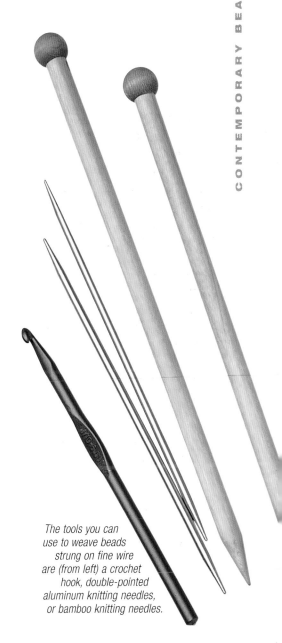

The tools you can use to weave beads strung on fine wire are (from left) a crochet hook, double-pointed aluminum knitting needles, or bamboo knitting needles.

The silhouette of these gold-and-crystal earrings recalls the roof of an ancient Chinese pagoda. Their airy cage frames, ingeniously wrapped, hold clusters of bead links.

Rachel Dow, Designer

Temple Earrings

MATERIALS

22 bi-cone glass beads in various colors, 4 mm diameter

22-gauge dead-soft gold-filled wire, 2½ feet (76.2 cm) long, for the cascading chain and eye pins

18-gauge dead-soft gold-filled wire, 1 foot (30.5 cm) long, for the armature

26-gauge dead-soft gold-filled wire, 3 feet (91.4 cm) long, for the wraps

2 dead-soft gold-filled jump rings, 18-gauge, 6 mm diameter

2 gold ear wires

TOOLS

Dowel, ½ inch (1.3 cm) diameter

INSTRUCTIONS

MAKE 2.

1 Make a chain of three linked wrapped-loop beads with the 22-gauge wire. Make eight eye pins from the same wire, slip a bead on each, and add three of these as dangles to the last loop of the bead chain. Attach two more to the next loop up. Finally, attach the last three in the next loop (see figure 1). Set this element aside.

2 Use flush cutters to cut two pieces of 18-gauge wire, each 3 inches (7.6 cm) long. Make small spirals on the ends of each wire. Center one piece of wire on the dowel and form the wire over it. Pinch the coiled ends toward each other while the wire is still on the dowel to make an element that looks like figure 2. Remove from the dowel and repeat with the other piece of wire.

3 Pair up the wires and wrap the 26-gauge wire three times around the apex of their curves. Push apart the two 18-gauge wires so that they criss-cross where they're bound together. Wrap the 26-gauge wire over the curves of the armature. As you come to a spoke, wrap it. Complete two full circuits over the armature, leaving a little space between the "rungs." To avoid distorting the armature's shape, hold the spoke that you're working with between your thumb and index finger. If the wrapping wire becomes bent or kinked, use chain-nose pliers to straighten it out.

4 Attach a jump ring to the frame where the spokes cross. Add the beaded chain element from step 1 to the jump ring.

5 Finish wrapping the armature, making a double wrap on the last spoke. Trim any excess wire.

6 Add an ear wire to the jump ring.

FIGURE 1

FIGURE 2

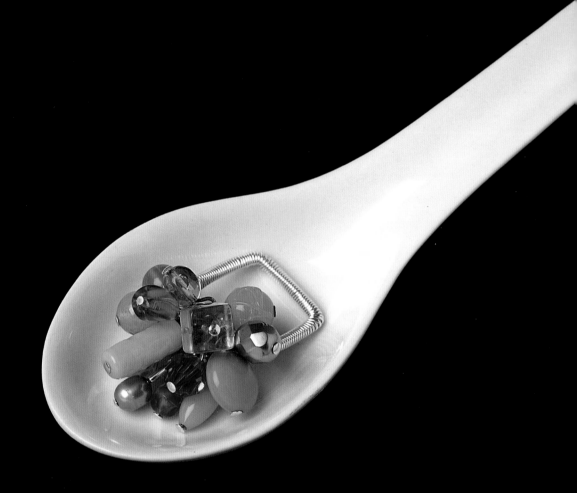

With every gesture, the beads on this unusual ring click together in a delightful way. Beads placed atop tube beads resemble a flower's stamens, and the color scheme feels fresh and appealing.

Spring Blossom Ring

Nathalie Mornu, Designer

MATERIALS

15 assorted green beads

3 assorted orange beads

3 silver tube beads, each ⅜ inch (0.95 cm) long

20-gauge silver-plated copper wire, 12 inches (30.5 cm) long, for the band

24-gauge sterling silver wire, 48 inches (1.2 m) long, for the wrap

18 head pins (20 gauge or size needed to fit inside bead holes), each 2 inches (5.1 cm) long

TOOLS

Small wooden board

Hammer

5 small nails

Masking tape

INSTRUCTIONS

1 Carefully measure the width of your finger at its base. Subtract ¹⁄₁₆ inch (0.2 cm) from that measurement. Draw a square with sides of that length on the board.

2 Make a jig by driving four of the nails into the board so that their outermost edges are completely within the lines. Hammer an anchoring nail a few inches away from one corner of the square.

3 Following the shape of the square, wrap the 20-gauge wire a few times around the anchor then tightly around the jig four times. As you wrap, keep straightening the wire by pressing against it with your fingers, and make the corners crisp by pressing them with the flat side of a pair of pliers. Once you've wrapped the wire, pull out two of the nails so you can remove the shape easily from the jig. Precisely trim the ends of the wire so that only three full wraps of the square shape remain. Use your fingers and pliers to true the shape of the square. Slip the band on your finger to make sure it's a good fit: it should feel only slightly loose.

4 Bind small bits of masking tape at the center of each side of the square wire form to prevent it from distorting as you work with it. Start the wrap of the 24-gauge wire at a 1 o'clock position, ⅛ inch (0.3 cm) from the inner edge of a corner. Tightly wrap it around the ring clockwise, keeping the coils as close together as possible; remove the pieces of masking tape as you reach each one during the process. Continue wrapping to just beyond the last corner.

5 As you wrap the last side of the ring's base, you'll create a series of integrated loops on which you'll later attach head pins strung with beads. Lay a nail along the edge of the partially unwrapped side. Wrap the wire once around both then carefully shift the nail so you can wrap the wire twice around only the band. Create six loops in this way. Slide the nail out from under the last loop, then resume wrapping the band.

6 Twist the wire ends around each other a few times, snip off the excess wire, and flatten the twist with the side of a pair of pliers. Straighten the loops so that they're parallel; if necessary, reshape them by reinserting the nail. Set the ring aside.

7 Place one bead on each head pin. Add a tube bead to three of the pins. To keep the beads on them, make a loop at the open end of each head pin. Attach trios of bead-strung head pins to each of the ring band's loops, working out from the center. Position the pins with tube beads on them nearer the middle, so that the shorter pins that are clustered around them will hold the taller ones aloft.

These delicate, lightweight earrings can dress up or dress down. Whatever the occasion, their design will be to your jewelry box what the little black dress is to your wardrobe.

Ellen Gerritse, Designer

Whisper Drops

MATERIALS

18 sterling silver seed beads

18 white-frost twisted tube beads,
  12 mm long

18 sterling silver crimp beads

18 sterling silver eye pins,
  1 inch (2.5 cm) long

2 sterling silver ear wires

INSTRUCTIONS

MAKE 2.

1 Slip one eye pin onto another eye pin,
  then a seed bead, a tube bead, and a
crimp bead. Close the crimp bead onto the
beaded eye pin, ½ inch (1.3 cm) from the end.

2 Add another eye pin to the element you
  made in step 1, with the same sequence
of beads and ending in a crimp bead.

3 Repeat steps 1 and 2 to make two
  more beaded elements.

4 Hang all three elements on an ear
  wire loop.

Like bubbles drifting down a river, beads float along a silver wire in this simplest of pins.

Silver Flow Brooch

Rachel Dow, Designer

MATERIALS

4 round glass beads, 5 mm diameter

16-gauge dead-soft sterling silver wire, 10 inches (25.4 cm) long

INSTRUCTIONS

1 Straighten the wire. Make a loop on one end to use later for making a hook for the pin stem.

2 Shape the wire to match figure 1, adding the beads as you work. After you shape the brooch, 1¾ inches (4.4 cm) of unbent wire should remain. File the end of this wire to a gradual taper for the pin stem, making the pin's point ¼ inch (0.6 cm) long.

3 To make the hook for the brooch, open the loop from step 1 with chain-nose pliers. Bend it at a right angle to the brooch.

4 Use round-nose pliers to bend the pin stem toward the hook. The pin stem should extend beyond the hook by ¼ inch (0.6 cm); make adjustments as necessary.

FIGURE 1

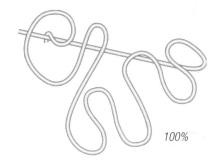

100%

Elegant twisted gold
wire frames a large
pendant of gleaming
amber, with a delicate
freshwater pearl
accenting the whole.
The designer was
lucky enough to find
a chunk of amber with
a tiny insect preserved
inside it.

Michaelanne Hall, Designer

Caught-in-Honey Pendant

MATERIALS

1 small freshwater pearl, 3 to 4 mm diameter

1 piece of amber, 20 to 25 mm diameter

1 gold bead, 2 mm diameter

24-gauge half-hard 14-karat gold round wire, 1½ inches (3.8 cm) long, for hanging the pearl

22-gauge soft 14-karat gold-filled square wire, 32 inches (81.3 cm) long, for the decorative wirework

20-gauge half-hard 14-karat gold half-round wire, 4½ inches (11.4 cm) long, for the wraps

TOOLS

Masking tape

Round dowel, 6 mm diameter

INSTRUCTIONS

1 Working with the 24-gauge wire and needle-nose pliers, turn ¹⁄₁₆ inch (0.2 cm) at one end and pinch it against the rest of the wire to make a tiny eye. String the gold bead and the pearl on the wire. Make a wrapped bead loop above the pearl.

2 Cut four pieces of 22-gauge wire, each 8 inches (20.3 cm) long. Mark the center of only one of the wires and use round-nose pliers to bend it into a U. Measure and mark ³⁄₁₆ inch (0.5 cm) from the bottom of the U and bend the wire 90 degrees there, to look like figure 1. Slide the pearl element made in step 1 onto the U.

3 Place the four 22-gauge wires together, side by side, with the U-shaped wire in an inner position. Cut two pieces of 20-gauge wire, each 1 inch

(2.5 cm) long. On either side of the U, wrap these three times around all the 22-gauge wires, making sure to keep them side by side as you wrap. Trim any excess 20-gauge wire, so that the ends are on the side opposite the U bend.

4 Holding the wrapped area gently with needle-nose pliers, twist both ends of the inner wire that's *not* the U wire.

5 Place one end of the amber against the wrapped quartet of wires and use your fingers to curve them against

FIGURE 1

Caught-in-Honey Pendant

FIGURE 2

Back

4 3

2

1

the stone. Referring to figure 2, hold your work so that the U-shaped wire is in the #2 position. Shape both ends of the twisted wire (#3) along either side of the amber piece. Snug wire #1 over the front of the amber piece, and wire #4 around the back. Shape wire #2 so that it gently curves no more than ⅛ inch (0.3 cm) away from the amber.

6 Collect all the wires at the top of the pendant, making certain that they hold the amber securely. Wrap masking tape around them, about 1 inch (2.5 cm) above where you will bind them. Cut a piece of 20-gauge wire 2½ inches (6.4 cm) long and, working from bottom to top, bind the wires together securely by wrapping the wire four times around them. Trim any excess wire on the back side of the pendant.

7 Remove the masking tape. Evenly divide the wires into two groups of four, making certain the group on the right side of the pendant contains two wires that aren't twisted. Arrange the wires in this set side by side, making sure the two outer wires are not twisted ones.

8 Still working from the right side of the pendant, twist the two inner wires. Use your fingers to shape the four wire ends across the front of the amber, then around the outside of wire #2. Hook their ends around wire #2 and clip off any excess wire.

9 Select two of the remaining four wire ends at the top of the pendant and bend them straight down over the back of the binding. Clip the wires ⅜ inch (1 cm) long. Turn under the ends and tuck them between the binding and the stone.

10 Use the remaining wires to make the bail. Twist the ones that aren't already twisted. Place the dowel behind them, right above the binding. Hold the wires against the dowel with your thumb and bend the wires slightly toward you. Wrap the left-hand wire away from you and to the left twice around the dowel. Repeat with the wire on the right so that it mirrors the left side. Remove the dowel and pinch the wraps close together.

11 Bring the left-hand wire of the bail down to wrap around wire #2, near the shoulder of the pendant. Clip any extra wire. Working from front to back, wrap the bail's right-hand wire twice around the top of the four wires that cross the front of the amber. Snip off any excess wire.

Wandering Gypsy Bracelet

Diane Guelzow, Designer

Eclectic, colorful, energetic—this bracelet's carefree mix of texture and bright shapes is just as fun to put together as it is to wear.

Wandering Gypsy Bracelet

MATERIALS

42 assorted beads (pearls, crystal, sterling silver, glass, polymer clay, bone, round and donut-shaped semiprecious stones, and large seed beads)

16-gauge sterling silver wire, 20 inches (45.7 cm) long, for the links and the hook

18-gauge brass wire, 15 inches (38.1 cm) long, for the jump rings

20-gauge sterling silver wire, 10 inches (25.4 cm) long, for the eye pins

9 sterling silver head pins, 4 mm long

TOOLS

Chasing hammer

Steel bench block

Dowel, ½ inch (1.3 cm) diameter

FINISHED LENGTH

8¼ inches (21 cm)

INSTRUCTIONS

1 Cut the 16-gauge silver wire into six pieces, each 2½ inches (6.4 cm) long; set aside the 2-inch piece that's left. File the ends smooth. Using the chasing hammer and working on a steel bench block, flatten the last ⅛ inch (0.3 cm) of the wire ends slightly.

2 With round-nose pliers, form side loops, facing in opposite directions, on the wire ends (see figure 1). Form each piece of wire into an S to create a link (see figure 2).

3 To give the links some variety, gently hammer the outermost parts of the loops on the bench block. If the hammering distorts their shapes, reshape them with round-nose pliers. Set the links aside.

4 Using the dowel and the 18-gauge brass wire, make 15 jump rings. Hammer them slightly, but if their ends spread apart a bit as a result, reshape them as needed.

5 To assemble the bracelet, connect the links with two jump rings between each. Add a single jump ring to one of the outer links to serve as part of the closing clasp. Set aside the remaining two jump rings.

6 Create the hook for closing the bracelet with the leftover piece of 16-gauge wire from step 1. File both ends smooth. Gently hammer the last ⅛ inch (0.3 cm) of the ends flat. Using round-nose pliers, create a small side loop on one end. Shape this side of the wire into a hook, then flatten all but the loops. On the other end of the wire, create a large side loop, bending it perpendicular to the hook. Use two jump rings to attach this loop to the last link.

7 Make three jump rings of any diameter you like out of the brass wire, and at least 15 eye pins from the 20-gauge wire, some with creatively shaped bead stops, such as spirals and wrapped loops. Slip between one and three beads on each of these, as well as on the purchased head pins. Trim and file the eye and head pins as needed. Attach beads to all of the links and the jump rings between them.

FIGURE 1

FIGURE 2

Ruby Wave Bracelet

Chris Orcutt, Designer

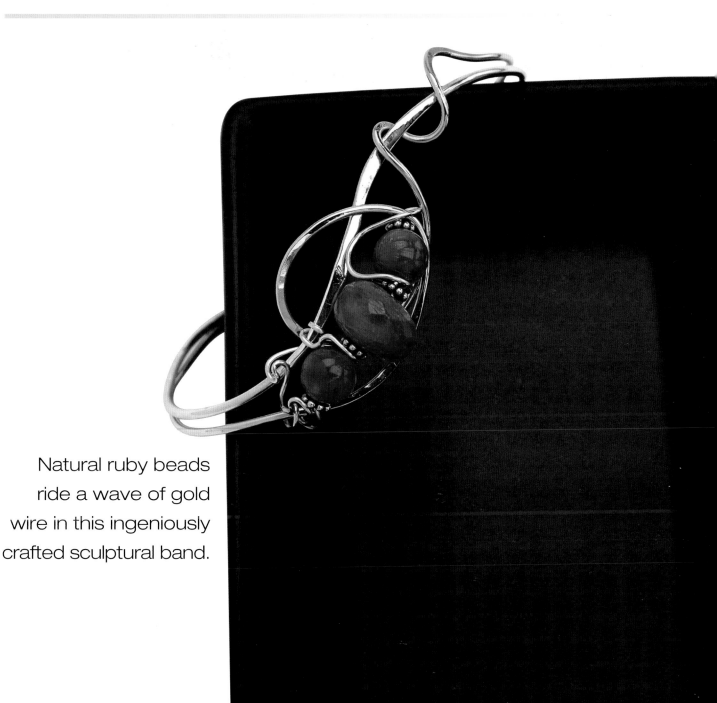

Natural ruby beads ride a wave of gold wire in this ingeniously crafted sculptural band.

Ruby Wave
Bracelet

MATERIALS

2 round natural ruby beads,
  8 mm diameter

1 natural ruby faceted rondelle,
  12 mm diameter

4 oxidized Bali sterling silver spacer
  beads, 2 x 6.9 mm

14-gauge dead-soft sterling silver wire,
  12 inches (30.5 cm) long

16-gauge dead-soft gold-filled wire,
  12 inches (30.5 cm) long

20-gauge dead-soft gold-filled wire,
  6 inches (15.2 cm) long

TOOLS

Ball-peen hammer and anvil

Bracelet mandrel

Plastic mallet

INSTRUCTIONS

1 Shape the center area of the 14-gauge wire into a gentle curve with round-nose pliers.

2 Use a ball-peen hammer and a jeweler's anvil to flatten the curved area.

3 Keeping one end each of the sterling silver and the 16-gauge gold-filled wires together in your hand, shape the gold wire into curves and loops over and around the silver wire, and use your fingers and round-nose pliers to wrap a large loop close to the center of the bracelet.

4 Once you're satisfied with the design, flatten a portion of the large gold loop as you did for the silver wire in step 2.

5 With your fingers or flat-nose pliers, twist the silver wire at the ends of the bracelet several times around the gold-filled one. Squeeze the bracelet ends (including the twists) with flat-nose pliers. Round off the cut ends with a fine file.

6 String the beads onto the 20-gauge gold-filled wire, starting and ending with a sterling silver spacer and using a spacer between each bead. Slide the beads to the middle of the wire.

7 Secure the beaded wire to the bracelet form with a few pleasing-looking loops, making sure to pass it between the spacers and the beads. Snip off any excess wire and tuck in the ends among the beads.

8 Form the bracelet over a bracelet mandrel and tap it into shape with a plastic mallet. Give the piece a final polish with a soft cloth or jewelry-polishing material.

Coppery Pink Flower Pin

Marinda Stewart, Designer

This glistening flower brooch is built on a type of pierced-dome pin back that's often used in costume jewelry. Loops of crocheted copper wire and iridescent beads form the petals, while twisted wire and the teensiest faceted beads make the stamens.

MATERIALS

65 pink oval beads, 6 mm diameter

30 pink crystal teardrop beads,
    3 mm diameter

24 pink faceted crystal beads,
    3 mm diameter

32 gold faceted crystal beads,
    3 mm diameter

1 pink pearl, 6 mm diameter

26-gauge copper wire,
    8 yards (7.3 m) long

26-gauge brass wire,
    2 yards (1.8 m) long

22 mm domed caging screen
    with a 4-prong mounting plate*

1-inch (2.5 cm) pin back

TOOLS

Crochet hook, 5 mm (size H U.S.)

Tape measure

Tetrachloroethylene adhesive,
    such as E6000

*Order from a supplier that sells
costume jewelry findings.*

Coppery Pink Flower Pin

INSTRUCTIONS

1 Tie a knot in one end of the copper wire to prevent the beads from sliding off. Randomly thread all of the beads, except the pearl, on it.

2 Leaving approximately a 2-inch (5.1 cm) tail, make a slipknot to begin. Crochet a single chain, with a bead in every stitch, to measure 40 inches (1.02 m) in length. To secure the stitching, pull the remaining wire through the last chain. Leave a 2-inch (5.1 cm) tail. Cut off the excess with wire cutters.

3 Make the first "petal" from a 3½- to 4-inch (8.9–10.2 cm) loop of beaded chain. Hook a folded 2-inch piece of wire through one end of the beaded chain. Bring the ends of the folded wire through a hole in the screen and twist them together on the underside. Repeat four more times, to make five petals in all, around the outer edge.

4 Repeat the process described in step 3 to make five 3- to 3½-inch (7.6–8.9 cm) loops inside the ring of outer petals. Set aside.

5 Make the stamens by threading the gold beads onto the brass wire. Tie a small knot at each wire's end, then gently fold it in half, arranging 16 beads on each side. Push one bead into the fold and twist the wire until the twist is ½ inch (1.3 cm) long. Randomly twist the beads into ½- to ¾-inch (1.3–1.9 cm) "branches" until the central "trunk" measures approximately 1¼ inches (3.2 cm) long, as shown in figure 1. Repeat for the other half of the wire, making a total of 12 to 14 branches. Trim off the excess wire from each end.

6 Gently coil the beaded brass wire stamens into a loose rosette. Attach the arrangement to the center of the flower, trimming the wire ends on the inner side of the dome.

7 With the remainder of the chain of pink beads, make a 2-inch (5 cm) loop, adding the pearl to its base. Attach the loop at the center of the brooch with a bit of wire; trim any excess.

8 Glue the pin back to the inside of the back of the domed caging screen's mounting plate. Set it aside to dry. When dry, attach the mounting plate to the domed part of the finding with needle-nose pliers, folding the prongs securely over the screen.

FIGURE 1

Santa Fe Cuff

Michaelanne Hall, Designer

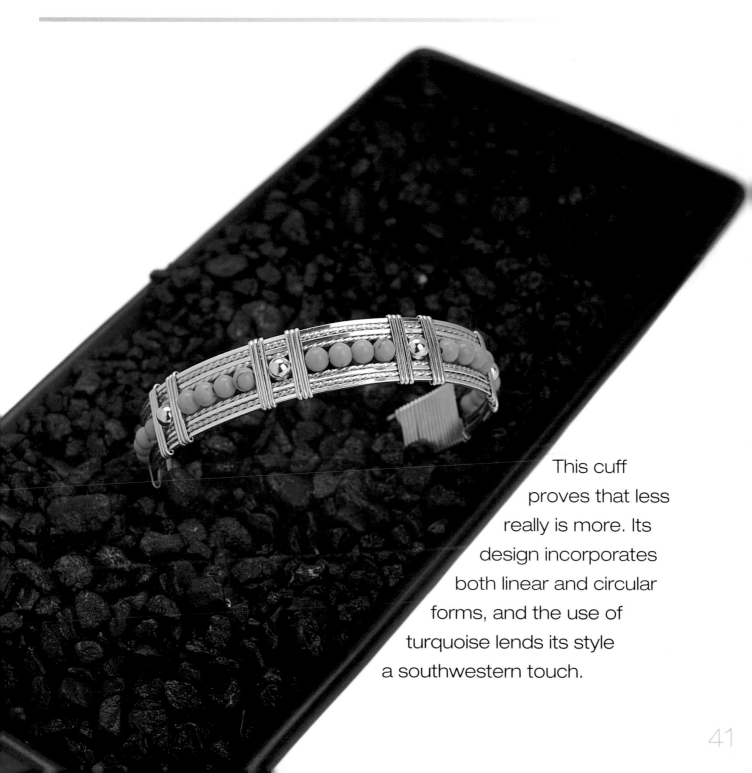

This cuff proves that less really is more. Its design incorporates both linear and circular forms, and the use of turquoise lends its style a southwestern touch.

Santa Fe Cuff

MATERIALS

5 gold-filled round beads,
4 mm diameter

24 turquoise round beads,
4 mm diameter

20-gauge half-hard sterling silver
square wire, 31 inches (78.7 cm)
long, for the cuff's exterior and
the hook

20-gauge half-hard 14-karat gold-filled
square wire, 26 inches (66 cm) long,
for the cuff's interior

24-gauge half-hard 14-karat gold-filled
square wire, 6½ inches (16.5 cm)
long, for stringing the beads

20-gauge half-hard 14-karat gold-filled
half-round wire, 46 inches (1.2 m)
long, for the wraps

TOOLS

Masking tape

INSTRUCTIONS

1 Straighten the silver wire, then cut one piece 15½ inches (39.4 cm) long and two pieces each 6½ inches (16.5 cm) long. Mark the center of the long piece with a permanent marker, center it in the jaws of flat-nose pliers, and bend both sides of the wire to make a U. Set aside these wires.

2 Cut the 20-gauge gold-filled square wire into four pieces, each 6½ inches (16.5 cm) long. Mark ½ inch (1.3 cm) from each end. Use a pin vise to twist all four pieces of wire between the marks, leaving the ends untwisted.

3 String all the beads on the 24-gauge wire, alternating four turquoise beads with a gold one.

4 Place the U-shaped silver wire from step 1 on your work surface; its legs will be the outermost wire of the cuff. Place all the 6½-inch (16.5 cm) wires between the legs and parallel to each other, alternating the twisted wires with the silver ones; put the beaded wire in the middle. Align the ends of the seven straight wires ¼ inch (0.6 cm) away from the U-shaped bend. Use masking tape to secure all the wires on each end, keeping the square wires flat.

5 Mark the interior wires at their midpoints. Center the third gold bead from the end on this midpoint mark.

6 Cut 10 pieces of 20-gauge half-round wire, each 3 inches (7.6 cm) long. Use needle-nose pliers to make a hook at one end of each piece.

7 Working directly next to the center gold bead, hook the sharp bend of one of the half-round wires over the silver outermost wire and, using needle-nose pliers, make three wraps around the bundle of wires. Trim it and finish by hooking the end to the inside.

8 Slide four turquoise beads against the wire wrap you just made and, using the same method as before, wrap a piece of half-round wire on the other side of the beads to frame them. Slide one gold bead against this wrap, then wrap another piece of half-round wire on the bead's other side. Repeat, leaving the last four turquoise beads on this side free. Repeat with the beads on the other side of the center gold bead.

9 Cut two pieces of half-round wire, each 18 inches (45.7 cm) long. Hook one piece next to the last set of four turquoise beads closest to the U-shaped bend in the silver wire. Wrap the half-round wire 16 to 18 times, until the ends of the interior parallel wires are no longer visible. Repeat on the other side, leaving the two outermost silver wires exposed.

10 Use flat-nose pliers to bend the outermost silver wires outward 45 degrees. Trim each to ⅜ inch (1 cm) long. Use round-nose pliers to roll them inward to make loops.

11 To make the hook for the clasp, cut a piece of square silver wire 2½ inches (6.4 cm) long. Bend it into a U shape. Using round-nose pliers held perpendicular to the wire, grasp the tip of the bend and angle it slightly. To form the hook, move your pliers to just beyond the angled tip and use your fingers to bend the wire ends around the outer part of the tool's tip. Now bend the ends of the wire outward 30 degrees. Mark ⅜ inch (1 cm) from each end and make a loop from that length of wire. Attach the hooks to the loops on the cuff.

12 Starting at the middle of the bracelet, slowly and gently shape its form until you can close the clasp.

Sassy Pin

Connie Fox, Designer

Make this eye-catching piece with beads that complement a favorite jacket, a knitted muffler, or anything that's big and bold enough to stand up to such sassiness.

Sassy Pin

MATERIALS

2 small beads* (the project uses a striped glass bead and a square hematite one)

1 resin focal bead,* 1½ inches (3.8 cm) long

1 plastic disk bead,* ¾ inch (1.9 cm) diameter

1 dotted resin bead,* ¾ inch (1.9 cm) diameter

18-gauge dead-soft sterling silver wire, 20 inches (50.8 cm) long, for the coiled element

14-gauge dead-soft sterling silver wire, 8 inches (20.3 cm) long, for wrapping around the focal bead

16-gauge half-hard or dead-soft sterling silver wire, 15 inches (38.1 cm) long, for the body of the brooch

The holes must be large enough to accommodate 16-gauge wire.

FINISHED LENGTH

3¾ inches (9.5 cm)

INSTRUCTIONS

1 To make the coiled element, place the 18-gauge wire across the 14-gauge wire. Coil the lighter gauge wire around the heavier one. Remove the 14-gauge wire. To form a loop that will allow you to attach the coiled component to the brooch later, use pliers to flip the last round on one end of the coil away from the rest of them. Do the same on the other end.

2 Mark the midpoint of the 14-gauge wire with a permanent marker. Use small round-nose pliers to make a spiral that ends at the midpoint mark. Repeat the same process with the other end of the wire, making a spiral oriented in the opposite direction from the first one.

3 With the tips of the pliers, push out the central section of both spirals (see figure 1 on page 47). Hold the component by its midsection, in the tips of chain-nose pliers. With your thumb and index finger, pinch the bases of the coned spirals together (see figure 2).

4 Use flat-nose pliers to stretch out the spiral to the length of the focal bead. Open the spiral slightly in the middle, insert the focal bead in one end, and stretch the wire over the other end of the bead (see figure 3). Twist the wire so that it fits snugly around the bead, then use flat-nose pliers to adjust the coil's spacing so that the rounds look even.

5 To form the spiral clasp, grasp the 16-gauge wire with flat-nose pliers, 1½ inches (3.8 cm) from one end, and make a right-angle bend. Grasp the long wire at the joint with round-nose pliers, holding them parallel to the bent wire (see figure 4). Start the spiral by using your thumb to push the long wire away from you, partway around one of the pliers' tips. Reorient the pliers as necessary to make a spiral with five revolutions, with the short tail of wire sticking out from the center of it. Grasp the long wire with flat-nose pliers where the spiral straightens out and make a right angle. Later you'll place the beads along this wire.

FIGURE **1**

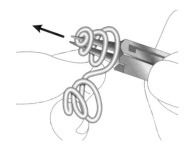

FIGURE **2**

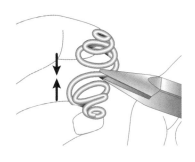

FIGURE **3**

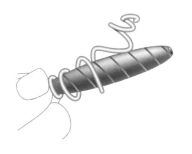

FIGURE **4**

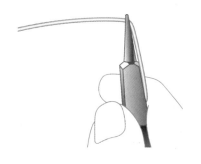

6 To make a hook to hold the pin stem, hold the center of the spiral with flat-nose pliers, with the long wire extending to the right, and bend the short tail up so that it almost rests against the spiral. Now grasp the short wire with round-nose pliers, close to the bend you just made; shape the wire back over the pliers into a hook. Cut the tail so that it extends ¼ inch (0.6 cm) below the spiral. Using small round-nose pliers, make a small loop in the end of it. Ideally, when you look at the front of the spiral, the clasp should not show at all.

7 Place the beads on the long wire, starting with the striped one; slide it close to the right angle to serve as a stop. Next, slide on a loop end of the coiled element you made in step 1. Add the caged focal bead, the other end of the coil, the hematite cube, the plastic disk, and finally the dotted bead. To withstand the rigors of opening and closing the brooch, this last bead should be a sturdy one.

8 Form the spring by holding the brooch so the front of the spiral faces you, with the opening of the clasp pointing up. With long round-nose pliers, grasp the wire 1 to 1½ inches (2.5 to 3.8 cm) away from the dotted bead. Make one and three-quarters revolutions perpendicular to the spiral, meanwhile making sure the end of the wire rotates under the spring.

9 To make the pin stem, put the working wire into the clasp. Cut the end of the wire so that it's just slightly longer than the clasp. File it to a point sharp enough to penetrate loosely woven clothing, but not so sharp that the tip can be bent.

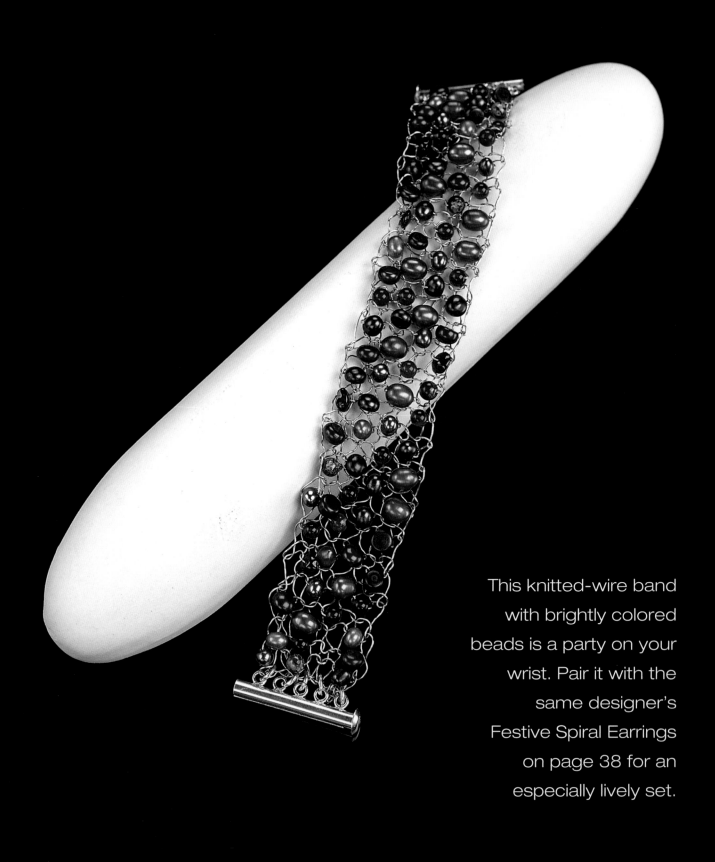

This knitted-wire band
with brightly colored
beads is a party on your
wrist. Pair it with the
same designer's
Festive Spiral Earrings
on page 38 for an
especially lively set.

Mardi Gras Bracelet

Rachel Dow, Designer

MATERIALS

95 gemstone and freshwater pearl beads in complementary colors, 4 to 6 mm diameter

26-gauge dead-soft gold-filled wire, 15 feet (4.6 m) long

10 sterling silver jump rings, 4 mm diameter

1 sterling silver 5-ring multistrand slide clasp

TOOLS

Knitting needles, 2.25 mm (size 1 U.S.)

FINISHED LENGTH

7 inches (17.8 cm)

INSTRUCTIONS

Note: Standard knitting abbreviations are used. After you have finished each row, pull the knitted strip down and reshape it. Make sure not to kink the wire. Use chain-nose pliers to straighten it out if you do.

1 Thread all the beads onto the wire.

Loosely CO 5 sts.

Row 1: K without adding any beads.

Row 2: P, adding beads randomly.

Alternate rows of k and p, adding beads randomly, until the band measures 7 inches (17.8 cm) long. The last row should be k without any beads added.

BO sts. Weave in both tail ends of the wire.

2 Place five evenly spaced jump rings along a short end of the band, slipping each ring through two strands of wire. Attach each jump ring to a ring on one of the clasp elements. Attach the other short end of the band to the other clasp element in the same way.

Make these gleaming post-
style pierced earrings in a
flash. Two versions are shown
here: one with pearls and
another pair made with paua
shell beads, both ingenious
interpretations of an
all-one-piece design.

Pearly Spirally Post Earrings

Hanni Yothers, Designer

MATERIALS

- 2 gray button pearls, 4 x 7 mm (or use paua shell beads)
- 22-gauge, half-hard 14-karat gold-filled wire, 8 inches (20.3 cm) long
- 2 14-karat gold-filled ear nuts

INSTRUCTIONS

1 Cut the wire into two 1½-inch (3.8 cm) pieces and two 2½ inch (6.4 cm) pieces.

2 Make a spiral from a 1½-inch (3.8 cm) piece of wire, until it's at least ³⁄₁₆ inch (0.5 cm) but not more than ¼ inch (0.6 cm) wide. Trim any remaining wire and file any sharp edges. Repeat the process with the second piece of 1½ inch (3.8 cm) wire.

3 Using your chain-nose pliers, make a 90-degree bend ¾ inch (1.9 cm) from the end of a 2½-inch (6.4 cm) piece of wire. This will be the earring's post. Thread one of the spirals you made in step 2 onto the short section of the wire, until it touches the bend, followed by a pearl (with the round side facing the spiral).

4 Use your thumb and middle finger (it's sometimes hard to hang on to) to grasp the pearl. Keep the long wire pointing up, pushing on it with your index finger near the bend in order to keep the pearl and spiral flush against the wire bend. With your other hand, grasp the long wire and pull it as tightly as possible over the top and down the back of the pearl. Wrap the long wire around the post wire, as close to the back of the pearl as possible. Keep each wrap tight against the previous one. Cut the wire when this spiral looks the same as the one on the front of the earring.

5 File any sharp edges on the spiral wrap and on the post that extends straight out from the pearl. File a tiny notch all the way around the post to keep the ear nut securely on it.

6 Repeat steps 3 through 5 for the second earring.

Beware of gazing at this chic ring for too long—the designer's sleek brass wirework is just as mesmerizing as its central pearl.

Hypnosis Ring

Joanna Gollberg, Designer

MATERIALS

1 half-drilled bead or pearl,
   4 mm diameter

12-gauge brass wire, 6 inches
   (15.2 cm) long

Extra-strength glue

TOOLS

Ring mandrel

INSTRUCTIONS

1 Make a 90-degree bend in the wire, ¼ inch (0.6 cm) away from its end. While holding the tail end of the bend in flat-nose pliers, completely wrap the wire once around the mandrel at your ring size.

2 File the tip of the bend to make the wire thinner, until it fits into the hole of the bead or pearl like a peg. Make sure to leave the wire thick near the crook of the bend, because you'll need to grasp it there when you make the spiral.

3 To make the spiral, carefully hold the peg with flat-nose pliers so you don't break it off. Use your fingers to fashion the long end of the wire into a spiral that's perpendicular to the peg. Continue until the spiral is the size you desire, then cut off any excess wire and file the end.

4 Put a small dot of extra-strength glue on the peg, then gently place the half-drilled bead or pearl on it. Allow the glue to dry.

Like an artist's squiggle, this bracelet's free-form wirework, wrapped onto memory wire, has a playful, intuitive quality. Have fun choosing not-quite-matched beads that can be unified by an overall color theme.

Amber Arc Bracelet

syndee holt, Designer

MATERIALS

Assortment of amber-colored beads of various sizes, shades, and shapes

24-gauge orange wire, 3 feet (91.4 cm) long, as the decorative wirework

Gold-tone memory wire, 23 inches (58.4 cm)*

Bead and glass glue or 5-minute epoxy

This is enough to circle a wrist about three times.

INSTRUCTIONS

1 Select a bead with a hole large enough to accommodate both the 24-gauge and the memory wire, put a dab of glue in the hole, and slip just the tips of one end of both wires into it. Allow the glue to dry completely.

2 String four beads on the memory wire; the last one should have a hole large enough to accept both wires. Slide the beads along the memory wire until they're against the glued bead.

3 String two beads on the 24-gauge wire and slide them along to the end with the glued bead. Pull the 24-gauge wire through the fourth bead that's on the memory wire. Don't pull the 24-gauge wire tight, but instead leave a small arc, along which the two beads can move freely. If you desire, you can alter the shape of the arc—for example, giving it a tight curve that stands away from the memory wire, or making several small bumps.

4 Repeat steps 2 and 3, randomly stringing different numbers of beads on both wires and making arcs of different lengths and shapes, until you've beaded all but the last ½ inch (1.3 cm) of the memory wire. Make sure the last bead has a hole large enough for both wires; put glue in the hole, and string both wires through it. Trim away any extra wire. Allow the glue to dry completely.

Like small whirlpools, silver links swirl around the beads in this necklace. The designer married a large turquoise pendant to a chain crafted entirely of handmade links.

Mami Laher, Designer

Vortex Necklace

MATERIALS

1 flat turquoise bead,
 1¼ inches (3.2 cm) diameter

6 round turquoise beads,
 1 cm diameter

2 faceted turquoise beads,
 7 mm diameter

18-gauge sterling silver wire,
 10 feet (3.1 m)

58 sterling silver jump rings,
 18-gauge, 5 mm diameter

TOOLS

Hammer and block

FINISHED LENGTH

17 inches (43.2 cm)

INSTRUCTIONS

1 Cut a piece of wire 6 inches (15.2 cm) long. On one end, make a spiral. Thread the large bead on the wire, then bend just the spiral around the end of the stone to cup the front of it. On the other end of the bead, make a wrapped loop. Cut the wire tail 1½ inches (3.8 cm) long and form it into a spiral. Bend this spiral to cup the top of the bead.

2 Cut four pieces of wire, each 3 inches (7.6 cm) long. Make four bead links shaped like figure 1, two with round beads on them and two with faceted beads on them. After you've finished the initial wire shaping, forge each link's curve at its apex, as shown by the wider areas in the illustration (if the link loses its form during this process, simply readjust its shape with pliers). These are A links.

3 Cut four pieces of wire, each 4½ inches (11.4 cm) long. Using a round bead on each, fashion bead links shaped

FIGURE 1

Vortex Necklace

like figure 2, forging the apexes of the curves, as shown. These are B links.

4 Cut 20 pieces of wire, each 3½ inches (8.9 cm) long. Shape each into a link as you did in step 3, but without a bead on it. These are C links.

5 To make the clasp, cut a piece of wire 2¼ inches (5.7 cm) long. Shape and forge it as shown in figure 3, then forge the outer curves.

6 Make half of the chain by joining the links with pairs of jump rings, keeping each one oriented as shown in the photograph. Use two jump rings to attach each link to the next, with the jump ring at the top connecting through the center of the spiraled area of one link and the curved part of the next, and the jump ring at the bottom likewise connecting the links in a mirrored fashion. Join them in

the following order: A C B C B C C C C C C C C A. The first A link should be one with a round bead on it, and the last A link should have a faceted one. Repeat to make the other half of the chain.

7 Place one chain on the work surface, with the links laid out in the sequence from the previous step. To its left, place the other chain so it mirrors the first. Keeping the chain pieces in this orientation, attach both of the round-bead A links to the wrapped loop of the center-piece, using jump rings through their spirals. Then use a jump ring to attach the forged curves of both A links together.

8 On one end of the chain, use a jump ring to attach the clasp. Attach the two remaining jump rings, one linked to the other, to the other end of the chain.

FIGURE 2

FIGURE 3

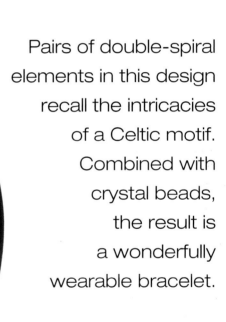

Celtic Crystal Bracelet

Marie Lee Carter, Designer

Pairs of double-spiral elements in this design recall the intricacies of a Celtic motif. Combined with crystal beads, the result is a wonderfully wearable bracelet.

Celtic Crystal Bracelet

MATERIALS

6 rondelle beads,* 6 mm diameter

16-gauge sterling silver wire, 14 inches (35.6 cm) long, for the spiraled elements

20-gauge sterling silver wire, 15 inches (38.1 cm) long, for the bead links

7 sterling silver jump rings, 16-gauge, 6 mm diameter

10 to 12 sterling silver jump rings, 16-gauge, 4.5 mm diameter

* The holes must be large enough to accommodate 20-gauge round wire.

TOOLS

Hammer and block

INSTRUCTIONS

1 Make the double-spiraled elements by cutting six pieces of 16-gauge wire, each 2 inches (5.1 cm) long. Flatten each end by striking it three or four times with a hammer. Make pairs of symmetrical spirals on each. Set aside.

2 Put on protective eyewear. Make a chain of three linked wrapped-loop beads with the 20-gauge wire. Repeat.

3 To make the hook, use the remaining 2-inch piece of 16-gauge wire. Make a large hook with a tiny loop at one end and a larger loop at the other. File any rough edges, then gently hammer the hook's curve.

4 Join pairs of double-spiraled elements by lining one atop the other and inserting a 6-mm jump ring through the centers of both. File any burrs. Lay open each pair, as you would a book, with the coils to the inside.

5 Connect the double-spiral elements with 4.5-mm jump rings.

6 Use a jump ring to connect the ends of the double-spiral linked chain to an end loop of a trio you made in step 2.

7 To make the clasp's eye, attach a 6-mm jump ring to one end of the bracelet; using a 4.5-mm jump ring, attach the hook to the other. (You may use additional jump rings to extend the length of the bracelet.) File any burrs.

Lucky Necklace

Mami Laher, Designer

The carved charm on this
spectacular necklace might
attract good fortune. Though
the bead links look ornate,
they consist of just
a few simple elements.

Lucky Necklace

MATERIALS

25 assorted honey-colored glass beads, 5 mm

4 dichroic glass cube beads, 9 mm

12 faceted beads, 1 cm

4 rondelles, 1 cm

2 flat stone beads, 1 inch (2.5 cm) diameter

1 round carved charm, 1¾ inches (4.4 cm) diameter

20-gauge gold-filled square wire, 49 inches (1.2 m) long, for the caged bead links

22-gauge gold-filled square wire, 48 inches (1.2 m) long, for the caged bead links

18-gauge gold-filled wire, 27 inches (68.6 cm) long, for making bead loop links

16-gauge gold-filled wire, 4¼ inches (10.8 cm) long, for the clasp and a connection element

28 jump rings, 18-gauge gold filled, 5 mm diameter

2 jump rings, 18-gauge gold filled, 9 mm diameter

1 jump ring, 18-gauge gold filled, 3 mm diameter

TOOLS

Tabletop vise

Hammer and block

FINISHED LENGTH

27 inches (68.6 cm)

INSTRUCTIONS

1 Cut and twist four pieces of 20-gauge square wire, each 8 inches (20.3 cm) long.

2 Cut two pieces of twisted wire, each 3½ inches (8.9 cm) long. Cut one piece of untwisted 20-gauge square wire 4¼ inches (10.8 cm) long. Slip two 5-mm beads on each twisted wire and one glass cube on the untwisted wire and place them side by side, as shown in figure 1, shaping the wires into bundles at the ends.

3 Cut two pieces of 22-gauge square wire, each 6 inches (15.2 cm) long. Clamp the end of one in the vise and wrap the other end four times around one of the bundled wire ends; repeat for the other end. Make spirals out of all six wire ends. Repeat the process to make a total of four caged-bead links.

4 Using the 18-gauge wire, make bead loop links out of each faceted bead, rondelle, stone bead, and the remaining 5-mm beads.

5 To make the clasp, use a piece of 16-gauge wire 2¼ inches (5.7 cm) long. Shape it as shown in figure 2, then forge the large outside curves. Adjust the clasp's form if the hammer's blows distort it.

6 To assemble one side of the chain, attach the links with 5-mm jump rings. For the caged bead links, pass the jump ring through the spiral of the center wire. The parts are assembled with faceted beads alternating a caged bead, a stone, a caged bead, and ending with two rondelles and two 5-mm beads. On the end with a 5-mm bead, attach the clasp with a jump ring.

7 Make a second chain, as described in the previous step, but on the end with the 5-mm bead, use a 5-mm jump ring to attach a 9-mm jump ring.

8 An extra length of chain will be added to the 9-mm jump ring. To make it, link together the five remaining bead loops by their loops. Use the 3-mm jump ring to hang one end of the chain to the 5-mm jump ring.

9 Cut a piece of 16-gauge wire 2 inches (5.1 cm) long and shape it to look like figure 3. Use the remaining 9-mm jump ring to hang the charm from the central loop of this element. Attach a chain through the center of each spiral with a 5-mm jump ring.

FIGURE 1

FIGURE 2

FIGURE 3

Love Knot Chandeliers

Andrea L. McLester, Designer

Shifting angles of view make dichroic glass beads come alive in these show-stopping earrings. The coiled area may look challenging to make, but it's actually as easy as slipping keys on a key ring.

Love Knot
Chandeliers

MATERIALS

10 disk-shaped dichroic glass spacer
   beads, ⅛ x ⅝ inches (0.3 x 1.6 cm)

8 saucer-shaped sterling silver beads,
   5 mm diameter

20-gauge dead-soft sterling silver wire,
   7 feet (2.1 m) long

2 French ear wires

TOOLS

⅜-inch (0.95 cm) dowel or
   other mandrel

INSTRUCTIONS

Note: The earrings' finished dimensions
are 1½ x 3 inches (3.8 x 7.6 cm); for
smaller-scale earrings, use smaller
dowels and add more turns to the spirals
on the crosspiece. Other components
should be adjusted accordingly, so you
may wish to make a sample earring using
an inexpensive wire first.

1 Create the Love Knot by wrapping a
   14-inch (35.6 cm) piece of 20-gauge
wire around the dowel 12 times. Remove
the coil from the dowel and trim any
excess wire from the ends.

2 Gently grasping the ends of the coil,
   spread it so that the sixth wrap is
exposed just enough to cut the coil neatly
in half with flush cutters. Be careful not to
spread the entire coil apart.

3 Carefully thread one coil through
   the other, as if adding a key to a
split-ring key chain. Once the coils are
entwined, spread their outer sides.

4 Cut a piece of wire 3 inches (7.6 cm)
   long. Using round-nose pliers, make
a small wrapped loop at one end. Thread a
dichroic bead on the wire; slip it through
the center of the Love Knot, making sure
that it passes straight through all its rings;
and add another dichroic bead onto it. Use
the round-nose pliers to make a long, oval-
shaped wrapped loop, ½ inch (1.3 cm)
from the last bead. This loop should be
long enough to hold two pieces of
20-gauge wire lying side by side.

5 Repeat steps 1 through 4 to make
   a second knot assembly.

6 Connect the knot assemblies to ear
   wires by their loops.

7 Bend a 3-inch (7.6 cm) piece of wire at its center, so that it's shaped like a U. Thread this wire through the oval loop on one of the knot components. Insert both ends of the wire through a dichroic bead. Trim each end of the wire so that it extends no more than ⅜ inch (0.95 cm) from the bottom of the bead. Shape the ends of the wire into a pair of small, side-by-side loops that are perpendicular to the large loop above the bead. Repeat for the other earring.

8 For the center dangle, make a spiral with a 4-inch (10.2 cm) piece of wire, stopping when there's just ½ inch (1.3 cm) of wire left. Grasp the end of it and make a small loop in the direction opposite the spiral at the other end. Open the loop and thread it through the pair of side-by-side loops you created in step 7. Close the loop. Repeat for the other earring.

9 For the crosspiece, you'll need a 6½-inch (16.5 cm) piece of wire. Use a permanent marker to mark the center of the wire. Make a spiral until you are ¼ inch (0.6 cm) from the center mark.

10 Thread the crosspiece through the lower loop of the knot assembly. Make another spiral at the other end. If necessary, use needle-nose pliers to pinch the lower loop on the knot assembly so that the crosspiece rests above, not beside, the wire holding the center pendant.

11 Repeat steps 9 and 10 for the other earring.

12 For the side dangles, cut a 2-inch (5.1 cm) piece of wire and make a small loop at one end of it. (If you wish, you may substitute manufactured head pins.) Use needle-nose pliers to bend this loop 90 degrees. Thread a silver saucer bead, a dichroic bead, and another silver saucer bead onto the pin. Make a U-shaped bend ⅜ inch (1.0 cm) away from the last bead. Thread the wire through one of the crosspiece spirals and then close it with a wrapped loop, making sure the pendant swings freely. Repeat this step for the other dangle.

This designer used bold glass beads and branching links to create an unusual geometric piece with lean, high-tech style. Despite the complex result, the necklace is actually quite simple to make.

Odyssey Necklace

Ellen Gerritse, Designer

MATERIALS

20 black pyramid-style stone beads, 6 mm diameter

57 sterling silver tube beads, 6 mm diameter

57 sterling silver crimp beads, 1.3 mm diameter

57 matte-gray Japanese tube beads, 3 mm diameter

6 assorted white glass beads, 15 mm maximum diameter

6 assorted red glass beads, 15 mm maximum diameter

6 assorted black glass beads, 15 mm maximum diameter

57 sterling silver eye pins, 1½ inches (3.8 cm) long

2 medium sterling silver jump rings

1 sterling silver clasp and hook

TOOLS

Hammer and block

FINISHED LENGTH

16 inches (40.6 cm)

INSTRUCTIONS

1 You will make three different strands. For the first strand, place the following, in order, on an eye pin: a second eye pin, followed by a black pyramid bead, a silver tube bead, and a crimp bead. Hammer the end of the first eye pin to flatten it, then file the rough ends.

2 On the second eye pin, slip a third eye pin, followed by three gray tube beads, a silver tube bead, and a crimp bead. As before, flatten and file the end of the second eye pin.

3 On the third eye pin, repeat what you did with the first eye pin. With the fourth eye pin, repeat what you did with the second eye pin. Keep alternating bead patterns until you've used 19 eye pins. Don't add an eye pin to the 19th eye pin, only a black pyramid bead, a silver tube bead, and a crimp bead. Finish the end of the last eye pin with a loop.

4 For the second strand, work in the same manner as the first strand, but with a different bead pattern. On the first eye pin, add a second eye pin, then three gray tube beads, a silver tube bead, and a crimp bead. Hammer and file as before. On the second eye pin, add the third eye pin, a white glass bead, a silver tube bead, and a crimp bead. Hammer and file the end. On the third eye pin, repeat what you added to the first eye pin in this strand. On the fourth, add a red glass bead, a silver tube bead, and a crimp. Again, hammer and file.

The fifth eye pin has the same beads as the first eye pin. For the sixth one, add a black glass bead, a silver tube bead, and a crimp. Hammer and file as before. Repeat the pattern, alternating white, red, and black glass beads on the even-numbered eye pins, until you have strung 19 eye pins together. As in the first strand, the 19th eye pin has no eye pin added onto it; instead, add only three gray tube beads, a silver tube bead, and a crimp bead. Finish the end of the 19th eye pin with a loop.

5 The third strand differs from the others only in its bead pattern. On the first eye pin and all subsequent odd-numbered ones, add a second eye pin, then a black pyramid bead, a silver tube bead, and a crimp bead. Hammer and file the first eye pin. As in the second strand, the even-numbered eye pins get an additional eye pin, a glass bead, a silver tube bead, and a crimp bead added to them, but the color pattern changes to red, then black, then white, and repeats as before, until you have strung 19 eye pins together. As in the first strand, the 19th eye pin gets no eye pin added onto it, only a black pyramid bead, a silver tube bead, and a crimp bead. As before, the end of the 19th eye pin is finished with a loop.

6 Open the first and last loops on all three strands. Attach all the first loops to one jump ring, and all the last loops to another. Attach one half of the clasp to each jump ring.

Designer Elizabeth Larsen evokes
an exotic sea creature with this
high-contrast necklace. Her elegant
method of wrapping snow jade beads
with tendrils of black, spiraled wire
makes a stunning piece.

Anemone Choker

Elizabeth Larsen, Designer

MATERIALS

148 round white jade beads, 6 mm diameter

84 round white jade beads, 8 mm diameter

36 round white jade beads, 10 mm diameter

20-gauge round sterling silver wire, 12 feet (3.7 m) long, for the jump rings

24-gauge round black wire, 134 feet (40.8 m) long, for the wrapped bead loops

1 fancy "wave"-style clasp

Hypo cement adhesive for nonporous surfaces

TOOLS

Knitting needle, 2.75 mm (size 2 U.S.)

FINISHED LENGTH

17 inches (43.2 cm)

INSTRUCTIONS

1 Using the 20-gauge silver wire and the knitting needle, make 274 jump rings. Link the jump rings two by two to make a chain 15 inches (38.1 cm) long. Attach each half of the clasp to either end with jump rings. Set the chain aside.

2 Cut a piece of black wire 6 inches (15.2 cm) long. Using round-nose pliers, form a loop at one end. Add a white jade bead to the wire, then form a second loop. Hold this second loop with a pair of flat-nose or needle-nose pliers and loosely spiral the remaining wire around the bead with your free hand. Fasten the wire around the base of the first loop with one full wrap, then cut off any extra wire. Use needle-nose pliers to secure the end of the wire snugly around the base of the loop and secure it with a dab of glue. Figure 1 shows the finished element. Repeat for each bead. Depending on the bead's diameter, you may need more or less than 6 inches (15.2 cm) of wire for each.

3 To attach the beads to the chain, start at one end of the chain. Open a jump ring in the first pair, slip on two 6-mm wire-wrapped beads by their loops, and close the jump ring. Open the other jump ring from the same pair, attach it to the same loops of the wrapped beads, and close it. Repeat for all the pairs of jump rings, first attaching half the 6-mm beads, then half the 8-mm beads. Attach all the 10-mm beads, then the remainder of the 8-mm ones, and finally, the rest of the 6-mm beads.

FIGURE 1

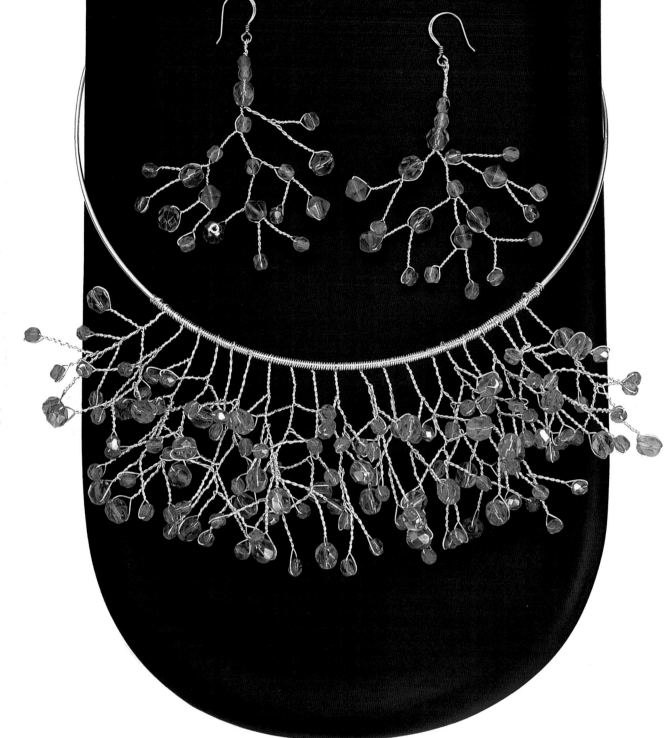

These delicate accessories
feature tiny turquoise facets that
shimmer on twisted silver wire.

Turquoise Twists Necklace and Earrings

Marinda Stewart, Designer

MATERIALS FOR THE NECKLACE

120 turquoise faceted glass beads, 4 mm and 6 mm diameter

26-gauge silver-tone wire, 10 yards (9.1 m) long

1 silver neck ring

INSTRUCTIONS

1 Thread all the beads onto the wire in random order. Wrap one end of the wire tightly onto the neck ring for ½ inch (1.3 cm).

2 With a permanent marker, make a mark 20 inches (50.8 cm) from where the wire comes off the neck ring. Fold this section of wire in half and slide the first bead into the fold. "Capture" it by twisting the wires together for approximately ½ inch (1.3 cm). Slide the next bead 1½ inches (3.8 cm) away from the base of the first twist and capture the bead by twisting the wire halves together for about ¾ inch (1.9 cm). Bring the next loose bead to the base of the last twist, create another twist, and create a "branch" there, as shown in figure 1. Working in turn with each loose bead on the untwisted wire, randomly twist beaded branches with two or three arms on each until you've used six or seven beads.

3 Wrap the neck ring tightly without beads for ¼ to ⅜ inch (0.6 to 1 cm). You should have used most of

FIGURE 1

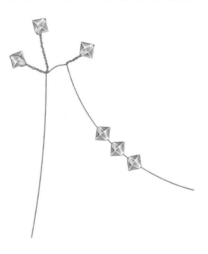

69

Turquoise Twists Necklace and Earrings

the 20 inches of wire that you had marked in step 2.

4 Repeat steps 2 and 3 to make a total of 18 branches. End with a ½-inch (1.3 cm) wrap as at the beginning of the ring. Trim any excess wire.

5 Arrange the arms so all the beads point down. If necessary, carefully slide the branches along the neck wire to center them.

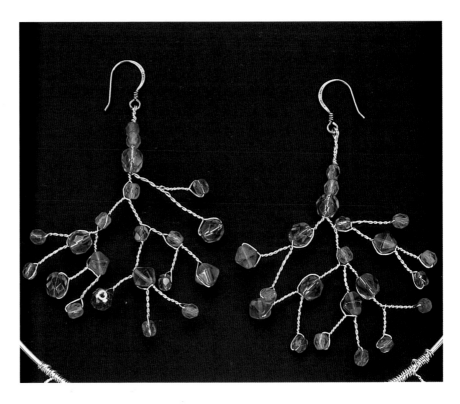

MATERIALS FOR THE EARRINGS

42 turquoise faceted glass beads, 4 and 6 mm diameter

26-gauge silver-colored wire, 48 inches (1.2 m) long

2 ear wires

INSTRUCTIONS

MAKE 2.

1 Cut a piece of wire 24 inches (61 cm) long. String 19 beads of both sizes randomly on it and knot the ends so the beads stay on. As with the necklace, twist the wire, with beads captured in it, into a pair of opposed branches.

2 Cut off the knots at the ends of the wires. Fold the branches together in the middle and twist. Thread a 6-mm and a pair of 4-mm beads onto this twisted wire. Attach an ear wire to the earring using a wrapped-loop finish. Trim any excess wire.

Quatrefoil Earrings

Eni Oken, Designer

Pearl, crystal, and rhinestone beads are transformed into a four-petaled focal point in these earrings. Sea-blue briolette dangles complete the delicate design.

Quatrefoil Earrings

INSTRUCTIONS

MAKE 2.

1 Form the dangle chains: cut three 3-inch (7.6 cm) lengths of wire. Slip one end of a wire on a ½-inch (1.3 cm) briolette, leaving a 1-inch (2.5 cm) tail. Bring both wires together and wrap the shorter end around the longer one. Trim the short end with a flush cutter.

2 Form a small loop with the round-nose pliers on the longer end of the wire, as close as possible to the previous wrap. Wrap the wire on top of the previous wrap. Trim the wire very closely with the cutter.

3 Repeat steps 1 and 2, using two of the ⅜-inch (1 cm) briolettes.

4 Form a quatrefoil: cut a 9-inch (22.9 cm) length of wire. Slip four faceted round beads onto the wire and form a circle, twisting the wires together, with a 2-inch (5 cm) tail on one side.

5 Bring the longer end of the wire between the first and second bead and wrap it once around that part of the wire that is holding the four beads in their circle shape; the first bead is now framed by wire.

6 Use round-nose pliers to wrap the short end of the wire into a wrapped loop, which is at the 12 o'clock position.

7 Repeat step 5 between the second and third beads. Create a wrapped loop to hold a ½-inch (1.3 cm) briolette dangle here. Figure 1 shows what your work should look like.

8 Repeat step 5 for the third and fourth beads. The wire has gone all the way around the circle of beads and is now back at the top loop.

9 Pass the wire behind the loop and slip on a small pearl, a rose-montée, and another pearl. Bring the wire across the quatrefoil (to the 6 o'clock position) and wrap it firmly around the shank of the loop that holds the dangle. Trim the wire closely.

10 Cut a 6-inch (15.2 cm) length of wire. Slip it onto the rose-montée and add a pearl to each side. Attach it to the quatrefoil by wrapping it once onto the right side, between the first and second beads, and once on the left side, between the third and fourth beads.

11 Using round-nose pliers, wrap a loop on each side, slipping a dangle made in step 3 into each loop. Trim the excess wire.

12 Using flat-nose pliers, open the loop on the ear wire. Slip the earring on it and close the loop.

MATERIALS

4 sea-green faceted briolettes, ⅜ inch (1 cm) long*

2 sea-green faceted briolettes, ½ inch (1.3 cm) long*

8 round faceted green crystal beads, 5 mm diameter

8 pearls, 2 mm diameter

2 lavender rose-montées (mounted rhinestones), 5 mm diameter

26-gauge dead-soft sterling silver wire, 4 feet (1.2 m) long

2 sterling silver lever-back ear wires

Briolettes are also called flat pears.

FIGURE 1

Arabesque Necklace and Earrings

Susan Campanini, Designer

Small companion beads in black and silver complement the pattern of these exotic lampworked beads. These beaded elements, paired with jig-formed wire links, create a design with Eastern flourishes.

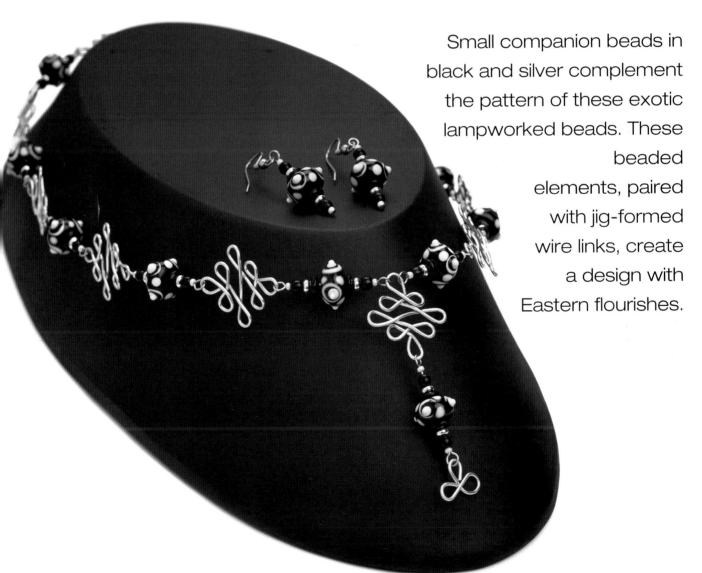

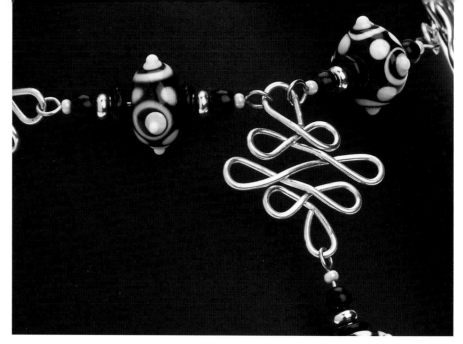

Arabesque Necklace and Earrings

MATERIALS

For beaded elements in necklace and earrings

26 white luster seed beads, size 11

26 black glass rounds, 4 mm diameter

26 silver-colored metal spacers, 4 mm diameter

26 black glass rondelles, 6 mm diameter

13 black-and-white dotted lampglass beads, 8 x 12 mm

18-gauge silver wire, 85 inches (2.2 m) long for the jig-formed links

16-gauge silver wire, 18 inches (45.7 cm) long, for the clasp

13 silver eye pins

2 surgical steel or silver French ear wires

TOOLS

Wire jig with 8 pegs

Knitting needle, any size

2 wood blocks, each 2 x 2 inches (5 x 5 cm)

FINISHED LENGTH

Necklace: 23 inches (58.4 cm)

INSTRUCTIONS

1 To make each bead loop link, slip beads on an eye pin in the following order: a white seed bead, a black round, a silver spacer, a black rondelle, and a lampglass bead (if the glass bead has a hole so large that it slips around on the pin, try putting a seed bead inside it before continuing), a black rondelle, a silver spacer, a black round, and a white seed bead. Finish the link with a loop. Repeat to make a total of 11 beaded links.

2 To fabricate a jig-formed link, place the pegs in the jig as shown in figure 1. Slip one end of the 18-gauge wire into the hole in the jig (marked with an X in the figure), then wind the working end of the wire around the pegs in the order and direction shown. Use the knitting needle to ease the finished element off each peg without distorting the wire's shape. Cut any extra wire off either end of the link; use round-nose pliers to completely close the outermost (#8 and #1 in the figure) loops at both ends. To flatten the element, place it on a wood block and strike it once with the second block. Make a total of nine jig-formed links.

FIGURE 1

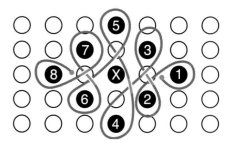

3 Attach five beaded links to the looped ends of four jig-formed ones, alternating them so that the chain begins and ends with beaded elements. Repeat, so that you finish with two short chains, each composed of nine links.

4 Link the two chains together by attaching an outermost loop from one end of each of them into an outermost loop of the remaining jig-formed link, which will serve as the top element of the necklace's pendant. Hang the remaining bead loop link from the opposite loop. Make a smaller wire dangle by wrapping the 18-gauge wire around only the first three pegs of the jig. Remove it carefully, then cut and flatten it as you did for the jig-formed links; hang the dangle from the free end of the bead loop link.

5 Make the hook and clasp from 16-gauge wire. For the clasp, make another wire element by following the directions in step 2. Fashion the hook in a similar way, but make one of its outermost loops longer by moving the appropriate peg out by two more holes. Squeeze the long loop to elongate and narrow it, then bend it with pliers to form a hook.

6 For earrings, make a pair of bead loop links as described in step 1, then attach them to ear wires.

Dynamic silver coils
hold a row of tiny
faceted beads in this
wonderfully simple
bangle that recalls the
ankle bracelets of India.

Marie Lee Carter, Designer

Rajah Bangle

MATERIALS

10 faceted round beads, 4 mm diameter*

14-gauge sterling silver wire, 8 inches (20.3 cm) long, for the bracelet's armature

22-gauge sterling silver wire, 80 inches (2 m) long, for the wrap

20-gauge sterling silver wire, 75 inches (1.9 m) long, for the wrap

The holes must be large enough to accommodate 22-gauge wire.

TOOLS

Pliers with plastic-coated jaws

Ball-peen hammer and block

Bent chain-nose pliers

Plastic mallet

Bracelet mandrel (a baseball bat is a fine substitute)

INSTRUCTIONS

Note: Makes one bracelet

1 Straighten the 14-gauge wire by gently pulling it through plastic-coated pliers. Use a ball-peen hammer to flatten each end of the wire (three or four taps should do it). Make a loop at each end with round-nose pliers. Bend them back a bit, to center them over the straight part of the wire. Mark the center of the wire with a permanent marker, then make a mark 1 inch (2.5 cm) from each side of the center point.

2 Put on eye protection to shield yourself as you work with the long pieces of wire. Starting at one loop, wrap the 22-gauge wire onto the 14-gauge wire. When you reach the first mark, thread a bead onto the 22-gauge wire, then hold it there as you make three more wraps. Add another bead and wrap as before, until you've used all the beads; finish wrapping the rest of the 14-gauge wire. Snip the end of the 22-gauge wire and press it into the coils with the bent chain-nose pliers. File any rough edges.

3 Wrap the 20-gauge wire over the 22-gauge wire. At the section with the beads, make two wraps between each bead, checking your work for uniformity. Finish as you did in step 2.

4 Create the hook of the clasp by prying open a loop on one end of the bangle with round-nose pliers. Grasp the hook with flat-nose pliers and turn it 90 degrees. Carefully file any rough edges. Slightly taper the tip of the hook.

5 With the plastic mallet, tap the bangle gently (avoiding the beads, which should face out) against the mandrel until it has a satisfactory shape.

6 Make sure that the hook fits into the loop that serves as the eye, gently twisting either as necessary.

The deep, iridescent jewel tones in this brooch charmingly capture one of nature's prettiest flying creatures. Colored wire skillfully ties together the overall color scheme.

Beaded Dragonfly Brooch

Carolyn Skei, Designer

MATERIALS

250 assorted seed beads in blues, greens, iridescent, and crystal

2 faceted iridescent beads, 4 mm diameter

2 round crystal beads, 8 mm diameter

18-gauge green wire, 20 inches (50.8 cm) long

22-gauge blue or purple wire, 20 inches (50.8 cm) long

28-gauge wire in color of your choice, 56 inches (1.4 m) long

Small pin back

Jewelry glue (optional)

INSTRUCTIONS

Note: Use pliers with plastic-coated jaws, or wrap metal jaws with duct tape, to protect the colored wire from scratches.

1 Shape the green wire into the dragonfly shape with round-nose pliers, using figure 1 as a template. Start at the head, making the first bend 1½ inches (3.8 cm) from one end to form the small V between the eyes. Shape symmetrical eye loops on either side of the bend, using round-nose pliers.

2 Make the U bend for the tail in the long end of the wire, 2½ inches (6.4 cm) below the eyes.

3 Holding the dragonfly body near its center, make the loop for the top right wing first, ½ inch (1.3 cm) below the eyes. Shape the other wings in a

FIGURE 1

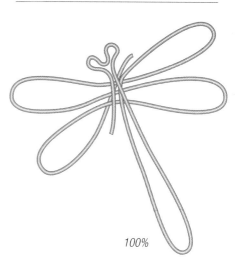

100%

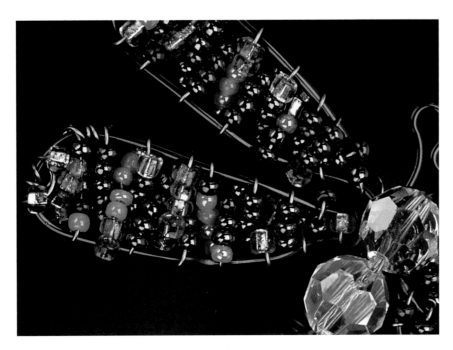

Beaded Dragonfly Brooch

figure-eight motif. Make the bottom wings slightly longer than the top wings if you wish. The wingspan should be 2½ inches (6.4 cm) when you are finished.

4 Push the wire's ends back toward the center of the body so they clasp the loose frame a bit tighter, but don't twist them. (You will wrap the body to hold it tighter in the next step.) Shorten the ends if necessary. Smooth, torque, and flatten the framework with flat-nose piers.

5 Using the blue or purple wire, hold the pin back against the framework, a short distance from the head, and wrap the thorax area from top to bottom. (Keep the pin back open so that the wire binds only the spine of the pin back.) Make a couple of X-shaped wraps where the wings intersect, to stabilize them, as you go. Keep the wrapping as neat and flat as possible. Check often to be sure that the pin back can still close.

6 Cut 12 inches (30.5 cm) of 28-gauge wire. Anchor one end near the base of the first wing by tucking it into the wire wrapping on the body. Wrap it once around the base of the wing, then add the first seed bead. (Spill the seed beads onto a woven dishtowel or other fabric to control them.)

7 Work back and forth across the wing, toward the tip, using a snug figure-eight wrap (i.e., over and under the frame in an alternating pattern). Add just enough seed beads to the beading wire to fill the space each time you wrap, snugging each line of beading against the one before it. Add beads in rows of related colors, occasionally punctuating the wing with one or two especially brilliant or sparkly beads. The outermost tip of the wing has two beads sitting atop the frame, with extra wire wraps. If you can, run the tail end of the beading wire back through one of the beads, then clip any excess. Use your pliers to put a tiny curve in the wire end and press it between the beads.

8 Repeat steps 6 and 7 for the remaining three wings.

9 Use the rest of the 28-gauge wire for the final embellishing. Fold the wire into a narrow U shape and position it under the body, just below the pin back; bring its ends to the front and twist them firmly together. Thread a 4-mm iridescent bead onto the pair of wires and push it down on the twisted wire, against the body. Twist the wires together several times until you have one strong wire that stretches to the neck. Add the two crystal beads onto the twisted wire. They should cover the area where the wings adjoin the body; if not, add another 4-mm iridescent bead before adding the crystal ones.

10 Wrap the two separate ends of the wire behind the neck of the dragonfly. Cinch everything together by twisting the ends behind the neck. Cut the excess wire, leaving ½ inch (1.3 cm) of twisted wire curved and tucked behind larger wires. If you wish, you can control the position of the embellishment beads and the wire ends with a small drop or two of jewelry glue.

Follies Chandeliers

Eni Oken, Designer

Beaded tendrils dangle from a larger bead that's framed by an unusual herringbone weave. The result is an airy design—daringly long yet light as a feather.

Follies Chandeliers

INSTRUCTIONS

1 Make the central dangles. Cut two pieces of 26-gauge wire 3 inches (7.6 cm) long each. Slip a ½-inch (1.3 cm) flat pear on each of them and use a 1-inch (2.5 cm) tail to make wrapped bead loops, trimming the tails' excess.

2 With the remaining wire and round-nose pliers, form small wrapped loops as close as possible to the ones you just made. Wind the wire on top of the previous wrapping; this gives the fine wire a more substantial appearance. Trim the wires closely.

3 Cut two pieces of 26-gauge wire 3 inches (7.6 cm) long. Make two wrapped loop bead links with a 9-mm rondelle on each, catching a ½-inch (1.3 cm) flat pear dangle at one end of each of the links. Trim off any extra wire.

4 Make the four side dangles, as you did in steps 1 and 2, using ⅜-inch (9.5 mm) flat pears instead.

5 Fabricate four smaller dangles from 4-inch (10.2 cm) lengths of 26-gauge wire. Make four wrapped bead loop links with two 5-mm beads each, catching a dangle from step 4 in one end of each. Trim away any extra wire.

6 Cut a piece of 24-gauge wire 4 inches (10.2 cm) long. Make a wrapped loop near one end of it, wrapping as many times as it takes to create a shank ¼ inch (0.6 cm) long. (Counting the number of times you wrap will help you replicate the shank on the opposite side of the bead.)

7 Slip a 10-mm rondelle onto the working end of the wire and make another ¼-inch (0.6 cm) shank with a wrapped loop on the other end of the wire, attaching the dangle you made in step 1 into the loop before you wrap it

closed (see figure 1). Trim the ends of the wires with a flush cutter.

8 To craft a herringbone weave around the 10-mm rondelle, cut a piece of 26-gauge wire 2½ feet (76.2 cm) long. Secure the wire by wrapping it twice around one of the shanks, near the bead. Trim the tail. Bring the working wire down one side of the bead, and clockwise around the shank, from front to back, positioning the wire as close to the bead as possible; do the same on the other side of the bead. This completes one entire herringbone weave around the bead.

9 Repeat to complete five full weaves around the bead. As you progress, snug the wire against the bead's sides.

10 Weave the top of a sixth herringbone, but before wrapping the wire on the lower shank, slip one of the smaller-bead dangles onto the wire. Twist a small loop at the 4 o'clock position. After weaving the wire around the lower shank, make another small loop at the 8 o'clock position for another dangle. Bring the wire to the top shank, wrap it tightly twice around it, and trim any extra wire.

11 Repeat steps 5 through 9 for the other earring.

12 Attach the ear wires to the empty loops at the ends of the shanks.

MATERIALS

2 deep-red faceted flat pears,* ½ inch (1.3 cm) diameter

2 deep-red faceted rondelles, 9 mm diameter

4 deep-red flat pears,* ⅜ inch (9.5 mm) diameter

8 deep-red round beads, 5 mm diameter

2 deep-red faceted rondelles, 10 mm diameter

26-gauge sterling dead-soft silver wire, 6 feet (1.8 m) long

24-gauge sterling dead-soft silver wire, 8 inches (20.3 cm) long

2 sterling silver lever-back ear wires

Flat pears are sometimes called briolettes.

FIGURE 1

Icy Drops Necklace and Earrings

Kate Drew-Wilkinson, Designer

This designer drapes crystal drops along silver chain in an earring-and-necklace set worthy of a big night out.

MATERIALS FOR THE NECKLACE

13 tapered faceted crystal beads, 4 mm diameter

21 round silver spacers, 2 mm diameter

1 faceted crystal drop, 13.5 x 9 mm

1 flat silver spacer, 6 mm diameter

1 tapered bell-shaped faceted crystal bead, 6.6 x 6 mm

7 flat silver spacers, 4 mm diameter

5 long tapered faceted crystal beads, 12.5 x 5 mm

17 silver saucer beads, 4 mm diameter

8 round silver spacers, 2.5 mm diameter

1 sterling silver melon bead, 6.5 x 2.5 mm

2 faceted crystal drops, 12 x 8 mm

2 flat silver spacers, 5 mm diameter

4 tapered faceted crystal beads, 6 mm diameter

4 faceted crystal rounds, 5 mm diameter

2 sterling silver seamless teardrop beads, 8 x 4 mm

2 faceted crystal rounds, 7 mm diameter

20-gauge half-hard wire, 15 inches (38.1 cm) long

1 sterling silver triple long and short 3.1 mm chain,* 15 inches (38.1 cm) long

1 sterling silver clasp

1 half-hard sterling silver ball-end head pin, 20 gauge, 2½ inches (6.4 cm) long

8 half-hard silver ball-end head pins, 20 gauge, 2 inches (5.1 cm) long

Triple long and short chain is composed of rectangular links alternating with three linked jump rings.

FINISHED LENGTH

15½ inches (39.4 cm)

Icy Drops Necklace and Earrings

INSTRUCTIONS

1 With a piece of wire 1¼ inches (3.2 cm) long, make a wrapped bead loop link with a 4-mm tapered crystal bead threaded between a pair of 2-mm round spacers; before closing the loops, slip the last link of one end of the chain on one, and the clasp on the other. Make another wrapped bead loop link for the other end of the chain. The free loop should be larger than usual, to serve as the eye for the clasp.

2 Put the following beads on the longer head pin: the 13.5 x 9-mm crystal drop, the 6-mm flat spacer, the bell-shaped crystal bead, a 4-mm flat spacer, a long tapered crystal bead, a saucer, and a 2.5-mm round spacer. Make a loop on the end.

3 Mark the central round link of the chain. Using a piece of wire 1¾ inches (4.4 cm) long, make a wrapped bead loop link, attaching the first loop to the central link of the chain; thread the following beads on the working wire: a 2-mm round spacer, the melon bead, another 2-mm round spacer, a saucer, and a 2.5-mm round spacer. Attach the head pin from the previous step to the second loop.

4 Put the following beads on a short head pin: a 12 x 8-mm crystal drop, a 5-mm flat spacer, a 6-mm tapered crystal bead, a 4-mm flat spacer, a 5-mm crystal round, a saucer, and a 2.5-mm round spacer. Make a loop to close the end. Repeat.

5 Using a piece of wire 1¾ inches (4.4 cm) long, make a wrapped bead loop link, attaching the first loop to the next round link over from the center of the chain; thread the following beads onto the working wire: a 2-mm round spacer, a seamless teardrop bead, a 2-mm round spacer, a 4-mm tapered crystal bead, and another 2-mm round spacer. Before closing the wire, attach the head pin made in the previous step to the second loop. Repeat, attaching this

pair of links on the opposite side of the chain, in the next round link over from the center one.

6 Thread the following beads on a short head pin: a 7-mm crystal round, a 4-mm flat spacer, a long tapered crystal bead, a saucer, and a 2-mm round spacer. Close the end by making a loop. Repeat.

7 Using a piece of wire 1¼ inches (3.2 cm) long, make a wrapped bead loop link, catching the first loop in the next free round link over from the center of the chain; on the working wire, string a 4-mm tapered crystal bead between a pair of 2-mm round spacers. Attach the head pin from the previous step to the second loop before closing it. Repeat, mirroring the placement on the other side.

8 String the following beads on a short head pin: a 6-mm tapered crystal bead, a 4-mm flat spacer, a 7-mm crystal round, a 5-mm crystal round, a saucer, a 4-mm tapered crystal bead, another saucer, and a 2.5-mm round spacer. Make a loop in the end. Repeat.

9 Repeat step 7.

10 On a head pin, thread the following beads: a saucer, a long tapered crystal bead, another saucer, a 4-mm tapered crystal bead, another saucer, and a 2-mm round spacer. Make a wrapped bead loop to attach it to the next free round link on the chain. Repeat, attaching this dangle so it mirrors the placement of the previous one.

MATERIALS FOR THE EARRINGS

6 tapered faceted crystal beads, 4 mm diameter

4 tapered faceted crystal beads, 5 mm diameter

2 faceted crystal rounds, 8 mm

2 long tapered faceted crystal beads, 12 x 8 mm

2 faceted crystal drops, 12.5 x 5 mm

30 silver spacers, various sizes and shapes

Silver chain, 6 inches (15.2 cm) long

6 half-hard ball-tipped head pins, 20-gauge, each 2 inches (5.1 cm) long

20-gauge half-hard wire, 3 inches (7.6 cm) long

2 silver ear wires

INSTRUCTIONS

MAKE 2.

1 Set aside six spacers and two of the 4-mm beads. Divide the rest of the beads into two identical sets.

2 Cut three pieces of chain, ranging their length from ½ to ⅞ inch (1.3 to 2.2 cm) long. Use three of the head pins and one set of beads to make the trio of dangles, stringing the larger crystals closer to the balled tip of each head pin, and stringing random numbers of spacers between each crystal. Make a wrapped loop at the open end of each head pin, slipping one end of a segment of chain onto the loop before closing it.

3 Cut a piece of wire 1½ inches (3.8 cm) long. Make a wrapped bead loop link, slipping all three of the free ends of the chain segments from the previous step onto the loop before closing it. Randomly string three of the spacers and one of the crystals you set aside in step 1 onto the wire. Before closing the other end, slip an ear wire onto the loop.

If you get starry-eyed over mystical dichroic-blue beads, you'll love making this adjustable bracelet. Tiny Bali spacer beads perfectly echo the wire's coil pattern.

Stargazer Armband

Hanni Yothers, Designer

MATERIALS

2 lampworked glass beads, 12 x 11 mm

5 lampworked glass beads, 7 x 11 mm

3 lampworked glass beads, 5 x 9 mm diameter

5 Bali silver spacer beads, 1 x 6 mm diameter

12-gauge dead-soft sterling silver wire, 10 inches (25.4 cm) long

18-gauge half-hard sterling silver wire, 24 inches (61 cm) long

TOOLS

Steel wool

Cookie sheet

INSTRUCTIONS

Note: The bracelet shown here has a 5½-inch (14 cm) circumference.

1 Straighten the length of 12-gauge wire by working it gently with your fingers or pulling a soft cloth down the length of the wire while holding one end.

2 Hold the 18-gauge wire tightly crosswise to the 12-gauge wire, with a ½-inch (1.3 cm) tail. Coil the 18-gauge wire around the heavier wire, keeping your turns as tight as possible. Pull off the coil, which should be about 2½ inches (6.4 cm) long, and cut it into four ½-inch (1.3 cm) sections and two ¼-inch (0.6 cm) sections.

3 File one end of the 12-gauge wire, grasp it with pliers, and wind it loosely around them to make a flat spiral ½ inch (1.3 cm) in diameter. Try to get the curved spiral to touch the flat wire that leads to the bracelet to keep beads from moving onto the spiral.

4 Slide one of the ¼-inch (0.6 cm) coils onto the 12-gauge wire and push it up against the spiral. Add one of the 7 x 11-mm beads, a spacer, and a 5 x 9-mm bead. Add the following elements, in this order: ½-inch (1.3 cm) coil, 7 x 11-mm bead, spacer, 12 x 11-mm bead, ½-inch (1.3 cm) coil, 5 x 9-mm bead, spacer, 7 x 11-mm bead, ½-inch (1.3 cm) coil, 12 x 11-mm bead, spacer, 7 x 11-mm bead, ½-inch (1.3 cm) coil, 7 x 11-mm bead, spacer, 5 x 9-mm bead, and a ¼-inch (0.6 cm) coil.

5 Trim the 12-gauge wire so that 1½ inches (3.8 cm) extend beyond the last coil. File the sharp ends of the wire. Grasp the very end of the wire with pliers and spiral it in toward the beads until it touches the last coil you added to the bracelet, making sure that this spiral is on the same plane but facing in the opposite direction as the first spiral. The spiral should be tight up against the end of the ¼-inch (0.6 cm) coil so that the coil can't move onto the spiral.

6 Use your fingers to gently bend the bracelet into a shape that is comfortable to wear on your wrist, keeping in mind that the spirals should be flat against the underside of your wrist.

7 When you have a comfortable shape, put the bracelet on a cookie sheet and place it in your oven at 550°F (287.8°C) for 2 to 2½ hours; the heat will harden the sterling and make it more springy.

8 Remove the oxidation caused by the heat by brushing the bracelet with steel wool under running water until you achieve the desired finish.

The dynamic spiral shape and brightly colored beads of these earrings are sure to attract attention at parties, or simply enhance an upbeat mood.

Festive Spiral Earrings

Rachel Dow, Designer

MATERIALS

- 10 pairs of round or button-shaped freshwater pearl beads in various colors, 4 mm diameter
- 2 pieces of 18-gauge colored wire, each 6½ inches (16.5 cm) long, for the armature
- 2 pieces of 26-gauge dead-soft gold-filled wire, each 10¼ inches (26 cm) long, for the wrap
- 2 gold-tone ear wires

INSTRUCTIONS

MAKE 2

Note: Match the sizes, shapes, and color patterns of the beads.

1 Straighten out the 18-gauge wire. Make a closed loop at the end of the wire. Grasp the loop with the widest part of a pair of chain-nose pliers and, holding your pliers hand stationary, rotate the wire into a loose spiral shape, leaving ½ inch (1.3 cm) of the tail end of the wire remaining.

2 Make another loop in the opposite direction as the spiral, with the remaining tail end of the wire. As you work, align it with the loop at the spiral's center. Trim any extra length of the wire that's left.

3 Secure the 26-gauge wire around the center loop in the spiral, slip on a bead, and tuck it into the spiral's loop. Hold the bead in place and wrap the wire twice around the spiral.

4 Add nine more beads, leaving a little bit of spacing between each one. As you work, make sure that your wrapping is tight and that the beads are snug against the spiral without distorting its shape. Straighten any kinks with chain-nose pliers. Finish by wrapping the lighter wire three times tightly around the base of the spiral's outer loop. Snip off any extra wire. When you wrap the second spiral, make a mirror-image earring by working on the opposite side and in the opposite direction as the first one.

5 Attach the gold-tone ear wires to the earrings' exterior loops.

Large copper-colored buttons function as beads in this glamorous, unusual piece. Its imaginative wire form, embellished with all manner of copper bits, springs fancifully into space.

Leaping Copper Collar

Ellen Gerritse, Designer

MATERIALS

7 mother-of-pearl buttons, 1 inch (2.5 cm) diameter

7 mother-of-pearl buttons, 1½ inches (3.8 cm) diameter

60 round copper spacer beads, 3 mm diameter

60 copper crimp beads

32 brown glass beads, 5 mm diameter

32 fancy copper star-and-moon bead caps, 8 mm diameter

18-gauge copper wire, 3 yards (2.7 m) long

Flat-link copper chain, 1 inch (2.5 cm) long

1 copper toggle clasp

2 copper jump rings

TOOLS

Bracelet mandrel or dowel at least 2 inches (7.6 cm) in diameter

Hammer and block

FINISHED LENGTH

17½ inches (44.5 cm)

INSTRUCTIONS

1 Coil the copper wire 15 times around the mandrel. Cut the coils apart, into perfect circles, with flush cutters. On each ring, use a permanent marker to mark a point opposite that of the cut ends. Set two rings aside; you'll use them later to attach the clasp pieces.

2 Line up all the buttons, alternating large and small side by side; the buttons' edges should just touch each other. Working from left to right, measure the distance between the right hole of the first button and the left hole of the next one. Divide this distance by 2, and mark one-half of it on either side of the center marks you made in step 1. Use chain-nose pliers to bend a ring 90 degrees at the marked points. Use the same pliers to straighten the wire between them.

3 Pass the wire "legs" through the two holes you measured in step 2. Repeat

Leaping
Copper Collar

the process until all the buttons are linked together in this way (see figure 1).

4 On each leg, push a copper bead, then a crimp bead, up against the buttonhole and use crimping pliers to close the crimp bead. Repeat for all the buttons.

5 Finish the end of each leg by placing one crimp bead, one brown glass bead, one bead cap, and one copper bead on it. Hammer the ends of the wire flat to prevent the beads from falling off, then file the ends smooth. Now push the loose

beads firmly against the flattened end of the wire and close the crimp bead with crimpling pliers.

6 Cut the copper chain into two parts of equal length. Attach one half of the toggle clasp to an end link in a chain piece with a copper jump ring; repeat for the other part of the clasp.

7 Slip a link from the clasp chain to the center of one of the two reserved copper rings. Use round-nose pliers to form a loop around the chain's link; the legs should cross each other now. Pinch

the ends of the legs together and slip them through the last buttonhole. Slide a round spacer and a crimp bead all the way down to the button and crimp as before. Repeat for the other end. Add a series of beads as you did in step 4; crimp the bead and flatten and file the wire end.

FIGURE 1

Beaded Channel Ring

Dianne Karg Baron, Designer

This dainty
ring can be worn
day in and day out,
with just about anything;
its classic good looks
are always right.

Beaded Channel Ring

INSTRUCTIONS

Note: You'll need enough wire to wrap the mandrel three times at the next-larger ring size, plus a bit of extra. You can use some string or a paper strip to find the right length.

1. Clean and straighten the square wire by pulling it through the rouge cloth. Tightly coil the wire around the narrow end of the mandrel, keeping it perpendicular to the tool as you go. To enlarge the coil, push it gently down the mandrel, twisting the tool as you work; periodically remove the coil, flip it over, and replace it on the mandrel, then continue enlarging it. Increase the diameter of the coil until it's one size larger than the ring size you wish to make. There should be three revolutions of wire all around it.

2. Use a permanent marker to draw lines where the ends of the wire crisscross. This line represents the bottom of the ring. Mark another line on the opposite side of the coil to represent the top of the ring. Remove the ring from the mandrel.

3. Thread the beads onto one of the wire ends and move them around the coil until they're positioned at the wire's midpoint. Wrap a piece of masking tape around the beads and shank to hold the beads in place. Measure and mark two lines, each ³⁄₁₆ inch (0.5 cm) long, on either side of the bottom line.

4. Using flat-nose pliers, grasp the shank parallel to one of the new marks. Bend one of the ends of the wire 90 degrees across the exterior of the shank, doing so at the mark closest to it, then wrap the wire around the shank twice. Trim it on the interior of the shank and press it tightly against the band, using flat-nose pliers. Repeat at the other mark with the other end of the wire.

5. Slide the ring onto the mandrel and apply pressure to even up its shape. Remove the masking tape and set the ring aside.

6. Using the rouge cloth, clean and straighten the half-round wire. Placing it at one end of the line of beads, and with the flat part of the wire facing in, wrap the wire around the band twice. Trim any extra wire from the inside of the ring, file its tip with a needle file, and press it flat with flat-nose pliers.

7. Repeat step 6 on the other end of the line of beads before removing the masking tape.

MATERIALS

5 round silver beads, 2 mm diameter

22-gauge soft square wire, for the ring's band (see Note, below)

22-gauge half-hard half-round wire, 2 inches (5 cm) long, for the wraps

TOOLS

Rouge cloth

Wooden ring mandrel

Masking tape

Chui Necklace

Andrea L. McLester, Designer

A bright mix
of shapes
and textures
abounds in this
African-inspired creation, which is named after the
Swahili word for "leopard." The chain, made from handmade jump rings, has just the right visual weight to
complement its spiraled-wire pendants.

Chui Necklace

MATERIALS

6 brown glass seed beads

6 sterling silver saucer-shaped beads, 5 mm diameter

3 vintage red glass spacers, 4 mm thick

1 lampworked cylinder bead, ¾ inch (1.9 cm) long

2 palm-wood bi-cone beads, each ½ x ⅞ inch (1.3 x 2.2 cm) long

2 lampworked cylinder beads, ⅝ inch (1.6 cm) long

2 round mother-of-pearl beads, 8 mm diameter

16-gauge dead-soft sterling silver wire, 15 feet (4.6 m) long

20-gauge dead-soft sterling silver wire, 5 feet (1.5 m) long

1 sterling silver toggle clasp

TOOLS

2 pairs of needle-nose pliers with non-serrated or plastic-coated jaws

¼-inch (0.6 cm) dowel or similar object to use as a mandrel

FINISHED LENGTH

20 inches (50.8 cm)

INSTRUCTIONS

Note: Adjust the length of the necklace if desired; it takes 6 jump rings, made from 16-gauge wire on a ¼-inch (0.6 cm) dowel, to make 1 inch (2.5 cm) of chain.

1 To make a handmade chain, make a coil roughly 3 inches (7.6 cm) long on the dowel with the 16-gauge wire. Remove the coil and use wire cutters to cut 116 rings from the coil's length.

2 Using the needle-nose pliers, close half the rings.

3 Thread one open ring through two closed ones.

4 Use an open ring to join a closed ring to one end of the short bit of chain you made in step 3. Close the open ring. Repeat this process until you've used all but two of your rings. Use the final two rings to attach your toggle clasp to the ends of the chain.

5 Use wire cutters to cut 10 pieces of 6-inch (15.2 cm), 20-gauge wire. Make 10 spiral head pins (the spiral technique is described on page 19); four full turns should be sufficient. These will be used to make beaded pendants.

6 Thread 1 seed bead, 1 silver saucer, 1 red spacer, another saucer, and another seed bead onto a spiral head pin. Using round-nose pliers, make a small loop at the top of this bead that is perpendicular to the spiral. Trim any excess wire. Thread the small loop onto the outermost wrap of another spiral head pin. You may need to loosen the last wrap a bit so the pendant can hang properly from it. Add the ¾-inch (1.9 cm) cylinder bead to this second spiral head pin. Make a loop at the top of this bead and trim any excess wire. Attach this jointed pendant to the center link in your chain, carefully opening the loop in the same way you would a jump ring.

7 Cut a 6-inch (15.2 cm) piece of 16-gauge wire. Create a large spiral on one end, turning it three times. Thread the spiral through the second link from the center pendant and make another small spiral at the top, turning this spiral one and a half turns in the direction opposite that of the large spiral. To make it more visually interesting, use your thumb and forefinger to make the straight portion of the wire slightly wavy, until this short pendant is 1¾ inches (4.4 cm) long. Make another wavy-wire piece for the other side of the center pendant.

8 Make two more beaded pendants as described in step 6, using bi-cone beads instead of cylinders. Attach them to the chain, on either side of the wavy wire pendants, skipping a link between them.

9 Make and attach two more wavy-wire pendants, as you did in step 7. If necessary, make additional turns to the lower spiral so that it's approximately 1¼ inches (3.2 cm) long.

10 Thread one of the smaller cylinder beads onto a spiral head pin. Make a loop at the top of the bead. Repeat to make a second pendant. Attach the small loops to the chains as before.

11 Make another pair of wavy-wire spirals from 6-inch (15.2 cm) pieces of 16-gauge wire, turning them each four times. Attach them as before, closing with a small spiral at the top. These pendants should be approximately 1 inch (2.5 cm) long. If necessary, make additional turns to the lower spiral to achieve this length.

12 Thread one mother-of-pearl bead onto each of the last two spiral head pins. Make loops at the tops of the beads and attach these outermost pendants to the chain.

Since every river-polished stone has its own shape and personality, tailor the way you wrap each one to enhance its individuality.

Rachel Dow, Designer

River Dance Bracelet

MATERIALS

5 tumbled river stones, 14 to 16 mm diameter

18-gauge dead-soft sterling silver wire, 12 feet (3.7 m) long

1 sterling silver chain-link bracelet with toggle, 8 inches (20.3 cm) long

At least 11 sterling silver jump rings, 4 mm diameter

FINISHED LENGTH

7½ inches (19 cm)

INSTRUCTIONS

1 Lay out the stones in the order you wish to place them on the bracelet, keeping in mind how their colors and shapes relate to each other.

2 Cut five pieces of wire, each 6¼ inches (15.9 cm) long. Leaving a tail 1 inch (2.5 cm) long at the top of the center stone, wrap the long end of the wire around it. Hold both stone and wire firmly as you crisscross the wire. Once you've finished, wrap the working wire twice around the tail, then form a wrapped loop. Wrap the rest of the stones.

3 Determine where to hang the wrapped stones on the chain; they shouldn't be too close to the toggle ends. Attach the center stone first, hanging it from a short chain made from three linked jump rings. Stagger the lengths of the other stones by changing the number of jump rings from which they hang.

The carved amethyst beads and golden fringes of these super-simple earrings evoke swaying paper lanterns of the Orient.

Kate Drew-Wilkinson, Designer

Lantern Earrings

MATERIALS

4 round beads, 14-karat gold filled,
  2.5 mm diameter

8 spacers, 14-karat gold filled,
  2.5 mm diameter

4 turquoise beads, 6 mm diameter

4 spacers, 14-karat gold filled, 4 mm
  diameter

2 carved amethyst oval beads,
  10 x 15 mm

4 round beads, 14-karat gold filled,
  2 mm diameter

2 turquoise beads, 4 mm diameter

22-gauge half-hard 14-karat gold-
  filled wire, 9 inches (22.9 cm) long

14-karat gold-filled 1 mm flat chain,
  16 inches (40.6 cm) long

2 gold jump rings, 5 mm diameter

2 14-karat gold-filled ear wires

INSTRUCTIONS

MAKE 2.

1 Cut six segments of chain that range in length from ¾ to 1¾ inches (1.9 to 4.4 cm).

2 Cut a piece of wire 3 inches (7.6 cm) long. Fashion it into a wrapped bead loop link, catching one end of all the pieces of chain in one loop and stringing beads onto it in the following sequence: 2.5-mm round, 2.5-mm spacer, 6-mm turquoise, 4-mm spacer, amethyst, 4-mm spacer, 6-mm turquoise, 2.5-mm spacer, and 2.5-mm round. Cut off any extra wire.

3 Cut a piece of wire 1½ inches (3.8 cm) long. Make a wrapped bead loop link with beads in the following sequence: 2-mm round, 2.5-mm spacer, 4-mm turquoise, 2.5-mm spacer, and 2-mm round. Trim off the extra wire.

4 Attach the two bead links to each other with a jump ring. Connect the ear wire to the shorter bead link.

You'll look perfectly regal in this knitted neckpiece. Colored wire sets off ruby-colored beads in this easy-to-knit design. Prior knitting experience is essential!

Marinda Stewart, Designer

Cleopatra's Collar

MATERIALS

Red teardrops,* 3 and 6 mm diameter

Red pearls,* 6 mm diameter

Matte red faceted beads,*
    4 mm diameter

Transparent red faceted beads,*
    4 mm diameter

Transparent red faceted beads,*
    6 mm diameter

Red pyramid beads,* 6 mm diameter

2 spools of 28-gauge red craft wire,
    each with a minimum of 20 yards
    (18.3 m) of wire

1 toggle clasp

*You will need enough beads to string
    80 inches (2 m) of wire.*

TOOLS

Knitting needles, 10 mm (size 15 U.S.)

FINISHED LENGTH

25 inches (63.5 cm)

INSTRUCTIONS

Note: The designer recommends knitting in the Continental, rather than American, style.

1 String 40 inches (1 m) of beads in random order onto each spool of wire. Leave the bead-strung wire extended 20 yards (18.3 m) but still attached to the spools.

Working with the 2 wires tog, CO 3 sts, leaving a 4-inch (10.2 cm) tail.

Rows 1 & 2: K.

Row 3: Inc1, k3, inc1, for a total of 5 sts.

Row 4: K. As you work the first st, slide a bead from the first spool into the first st. For the next st, pull a bead from the second spool. Continue to alternate a bead from each spool with every st.

K every row until the work measures 19 inches (48.3 cm) long.

K 1 row without any beads.

For the next row, dec1, k3, dec1, to make 3 sts.

K for 2 rows.

BO. Cut all of the extra wire, leaving 4-inch (10.2 cm) tails.

2 Secure each wire end to one half of the toggle by wrapping it repeatedly through the first row of stitches and through the toggle's loop. Weave any excess wire through the work; bury the ends in the stitches.

3 Contour the necklace to your neck by compressing the stitches on the inside edge and stretching those on the outer edge.

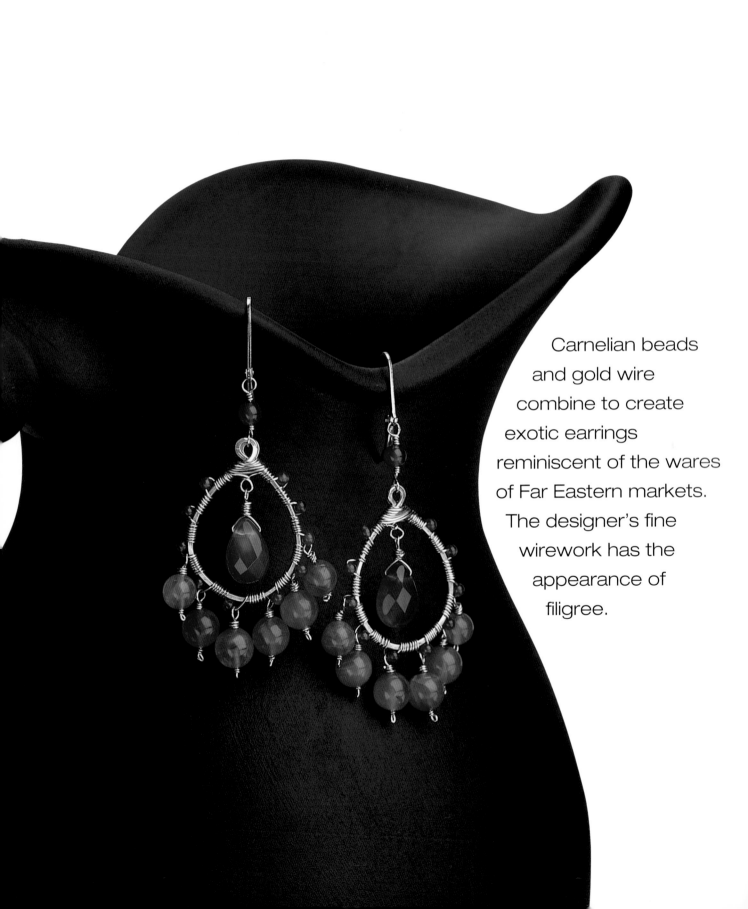

Carnelian beads and gold wire combine to create exotic earrings reminiscent of the wares of Far Eastern markets. The designer's fine wirework has the appearance of filigree.

Bollywood Dreams

Eni Oken, Designer

MATERIALS

12 round beads, 7 mm diameter

2 top-drilled faceted flat pear carnelian beads,* ½ inch (1.3 cm) long

20 round carnelian seed beads, 3 mm diameter

2 round carnelian beads, 5 mm diameter

26-gauge gold-filled dead-soft wire, 9 feet (2.7 m) long, for the wraps

18-gauge gold-filled dead-soft wire, 7½ inches (19 cm) long, for the teardrop-shaped element

2 gold-filled lever-back ear wires

* Faceted flat pear beads are sometimes called briolettes.

TOOLS

Wooden dowel or pen, ¾ inch (1.9 cm) diameter

Mallet or hammer

Anvil

INSTRUCTIONS

MAKE 2.

1 Cut 6 pieces of 26-gauge wire, each 3 inches (7.6 cm) long. Make eye pins with tiny wrapped loops out of each of them, then slip a 7-mm round bead onto each. Close the open ends with another miniscule wrapped loop. Cut off any excess wire.

2 Cut the 18-gauge wire in half. Working with one piece, form small loops at both ends of it. Using the wooden dowel and your fingers, form the wire into a teardrop shape. Flatten the shape on an anvil with a mallet or hammer until it's work hardened.

3 To create the flat-pear dangles at the earring's center, cut a piece of 26-gauge wire, 3 inches (7.6 cm) long. Place a flat pear on it, leaving a tail 1 inch (2.5 cm) long on one side; wrap the shorter wire around the longer one several times. Trim the short end of the wire. Now use round-nose pliers to form a small wrapped loop from the remaining wire, making the loop as close as possible to the wrapping you just did and winding some of the excess wire on top of the existing wrapping. Trim the wire closely.

4 To assemble all the elements, cut a piece of 26-gauge wire 2½ feet (76.2 cm) long. Leaving a 1-inch-long (2.5 cm) tail to help you hold onto it, start at one of the loops on the teardrop shape and tightly coil the wire to one of the loops

for ¼ inch (0.6 cm); trim the tail. Slip a seed bead onto the working wire, making sure the bead is positioned at the outermost edge of the wire teardrop, and continue coiling another ³⁄₁₆ inch (0.5 cm). Add another seed bead to the working wire and coil another ³⁄₁₆ inch (0.5 cm). Now slip a seed bead and one of the dangles you made in step 1 onto the working wire. Continue to wrap the wire and add the seed beads and dangles in this way until you've attached them all. After you finish, if the beads aren't symmetrically spaced on the teardrop, spread out the coils a bit until they are.

5 Bring together the two loops of the teardrop element so that one is atop the other, then wrap them together twice tightly. Form a small cap by wrapping the shoulders of the teardrop, below the loops, six more times. On the last wrap, slip the flat pear dangle onto the working wire, then use round-nose pliers to twist a small wrapped loop that faces into the center of the teardrop shape. Finish by tightly coiling it around the teardrop wire, near the cap. Trim any excess wire.

6 Using a 3-inch (7.6 cm) length of 26-gauge wire and a 5-mm bead, make a wrapped bead loop link that connects one of its loop to the two joined loops above the cap, and the other one in an ear wire.

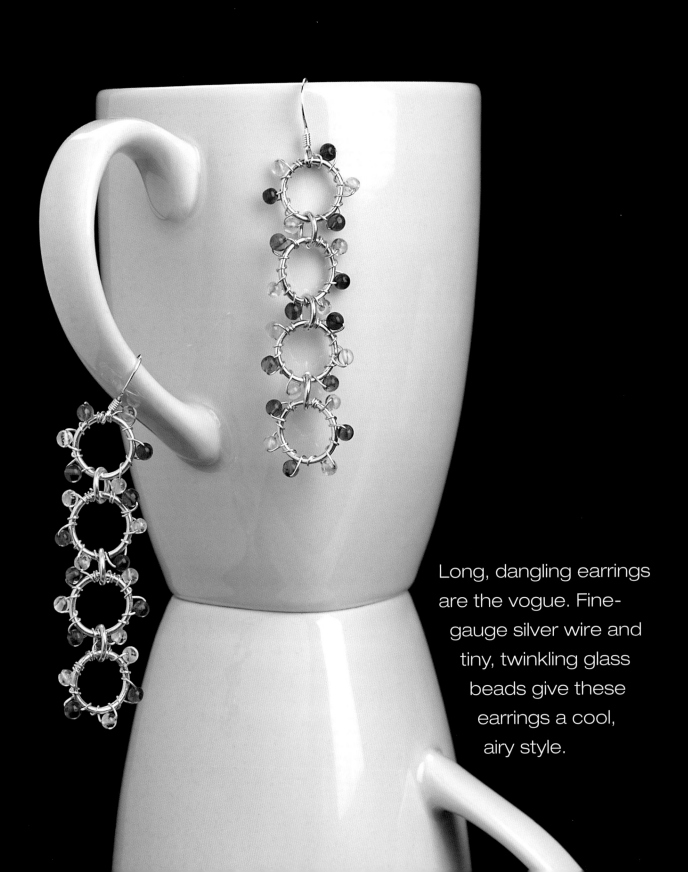

Long, dangling earrings are the vogue. Fine-gauge silver wire and tiny, twinkling glass beads give these earrings a cool, airy style.

Rachel Dow, Designer

Confetti Hoops

MATERIALS

48 gemstone beads in various colors, 3 to 4 mm diameter

26-gauge dead-soft sterling silver wire, 4 feet (1.2 m) long

8 jump rings, 16-gauge sterling silver, 10 mm diameter

6 jump rings, 18-gauge sterling silver, 6 mm diameter

2 sterling silver ear wires

INSTRUCTIONS

MAKE 2.

1 Using flush cutters, cut four pieces of 26-gauge wire, each 5¼ inches (13.3 cm) long.

2 Wrap one piece of 26-gauge wire twice around a 10-mm jump ring to secure it; using chain-nose pliers to grasp the thinner wire will help you get a tight wrap. Add a bead to the wire, hold it in place on the outer edge of the 10-mm jump ring, and wrap the wire tightly around the jump ring twice, being careful not to kink the light wire as you work.

3 Add another bead to the wire and continue wrapping and adding beads, working your way around the jump ring until you've attached six evenly spaced beads to it. Secure the tail of the wire by wrapping it tightly twice around the jump ring, close to the point where you began the wrapping. Cut off any extra wire.

4 Repeat steps 2 and 3 to make a total of four bead-wrapped 10-mm jump rings.

5 Use a fingernail or the tip of chain-nose pliers to separate the beginning/end wraps of wire on one of the bead-wrapped jump rings, and attach an ear wire there.

6 Using three 6-mm jump rings, link three more bead-wrapped jump rings sequentially to the one with the ear wire.

The chunky millefiori glass beads on this necklace evoke Old World charm. Wrapped loops of heavy wire echo the patterns on the ornate bead caps.

Kate Drew-Wilkinson, Designer

Venetian Reverie Necklace

MATERIALS

18 silver beads, 2.5 mm diameter

9 lampworked glass beads, 16 mm diameter

18-gauge half-hard sterling silver wire, 3 feet (91.4 cm) long

18-gauge sterling silver chain with 6 x 8 mm links, 8 inches (20.3 cm) long

18 silver bead caps, 10 mm diameter

Large heart-shaped silver toggle clasp

FINISHED LENGTH

25½ inches (64.8 cm)

INSTRUCTIONS

1 Cut every third link of the chain to free a pair of links, until you have eight pairs of chain links.

2 Using the wire, make a wrapped bead loop link, attaching one half of the toggle clasp to the loop before closing it. String the link with a silver bead, a bead cap, a glass bead, another bead cap, and a silver bead. Add a pair of chain links to the second loop before you close it. Cut off the remaining wire.

3 Make another wrapped bead loop link, slipping the free chain link from the previous step into the loop before closing it. String the link with beads, as described in step 2, and again add a pair of chain links to the second loop before you close it. Trim the remaining wire. Repeat until you've used all the beads. Add the other half of the toggle clasp to the last loop before closing it.

Like fire personified, this dynamic
pendant explores the entire warm
color range. Be sure to finish it with a
silk ribbon that does it justice.

Ronda Kivett, Designer

Flame Pendant

MATERIALS

20 red glass seed beads, size 6/0

1 small tube of matte orange glass seed beads, size 11/0

3 red glass tube beads, 14 x 4 mm

2 red round glass beads, 6 mm diameter

45–55 pink (of various shades) glass seed beads, size 6/0

18-gauge silver-tone wire, 8½ inches (21.6 cm) long, for the armature

24-gauge red wire, 3 yards (2.7 m) long, for the wraps

¾-inch (1.9 cm) wide silk ribbon, 27 inches (68.6 cm) long

INSTRUCTIONS

1 To create the armature, form the 18-gauge wire, using figure 1 as a template. At the top of the armature, make the loop twist sideways, rather than toward the front, so that the pendant will face forward when it hangs from the ribbon.

2 Cut a piece of 24-gauge wire 1 yard (91.4 cm) long. To secure it, wrap one end three or four times around the lower left corner of the triangular part of the armature.

3 String one red 6/0 seed bead, one orange seed bead, and another red 6/0 seed bead onto the 24-gauge wire; holding the beads along the exterior of the armature, wrap the lighter wire twice around the armature to secure them. This creates a "picot." Repeat four times, working from the bottom left corner of the triangle to the loop at the top of the armature.

4 Wrap the 24-gauge wire, with no beads on it, six times around the

FIGURE **1**

100%

Flame Pendant

base of the loop, then continue all along the loop itself.

5 Working from the base of the loop to the bottom right corner of the triangle, repeat step 3 to make five picots on the armature. Wrap the remaining 24-gauge wire around the wire along the baseline of the triangular shape, then trim any excess.

6 Cut another piece of 24-gauge wire, 1 yard (91.4 cm) long. Securely wrap one end of it four times between the third and fourth picots you made in step 3. String one tube bead on the wire, then wrap the wire tightly between the second and third picots you made in step 5. String another tube bead on the wire, then wrap the wire tightly around the center of the base of the triangular shape. String the last tube bead onto the wire, then wrap the wire tightly in the same place you first secured it. Don't trim the wire.

7 Use a random selection of beads for the rest of the triangular shape—but not the spirals at the pendant's bottom. As needed to fill in gaps, string short sections of pink and orange seed beads onto the remaining 24-gauge wire; wrap it around a picot or the armature to hold the beads in place. When you're finished, secure the wire around the form and trim off any extra material.

8 Cut a piece of 24-gauge wire 15 inches (38.1 cm) long. Secure one end to one of the spirals at the bottom, close to the corner of the triangle. String an orange seed bead onto the wire, hold the bead inside the curve of the spiral, and wrap the wire around the armature to hold the bead in position. Working toward the center, repeat to fill the exterior part of the spiral's curve with orange beads. Wrap the rest of the spiral with the light wire until you reach its center.

9 String one 6-mm bead onto the wire, hold it to the center of the spiral, and secure it to the armature. Bring the wire back around and through the bead's hole again; string six orange seed beads, then secure the wire near the spot where it went into the bead so that the orange beads form a halo around the outer half of the 6-mm bead. Trim any excess wire.

10 Using another piece of 24-gauge wire 15 inches (38.1 cm) long, bead the other spiral, mirroring the beading done on the first one.

11 Thread the ribbon on the pendant's loop with half the length on each side. Knot it close to either side of the loop to keep it on. As a decorative accent, add evenly spaced knots along the length of the ribbon.

Pearl-Set Ring

Dianne Karg Baron, Designer

Using a clever mock-prong setting, this delicate ring shows off a single pearl bead as if it were a precious gem.

Pearl-Set Ring

MATERIALS

1 pearl, 6 mm diameter

22-gauge soft square wire, 12 inches (30.5 cm) long, for the band

20-gauge half-hard half-round wire, 6 inches (15.2 cm) long, for the wraps

24-gauge soft wire, 4 inches (10.2 cm), for attaching the bead

TOOLS

Masking tape

Wooden ring mandrel

Rouge cloth

INSTRUCTIONS

1 Wrap a piece of masking tape one and a half times around the ring mandrel at one size larger than the desired finished size. Mark a vertical line on the tape at the point where it overlaps itself. Peel up enough of the top layer of tape so that you can transfer the line onto the bottom layer of tape as well. Remove the tape from the ring mandrel and place the tape on a work surface. Measure and mark the midpoint between the two lines, then draw lines ³⁄₁₆ inch (0.5 cm) on either side of that.

2 Using the rouge cloth, clean and straighten the square wire. Cut it exactly in half. Align both pieces of wire together, tape the ends, and measure and mark the midpoint of the bundle. Line up the midpoint of the tape with the midpoint of the wires, then transfer all five lines from the tape to the wire. Remove the tape from the wires.

3 At the outer marks, fold each wire inward so that their ends meet at the center. If the wires overlap, trim them flush.

4 Put the wires together, side by side; the ends should be next to each other on the inside. To create a flat shank four strands wide, tape both ends.

5 Bind the shank with the half-round wire, wrapping the entire section between the two inner marks. Start and end the wrapping so that the cut ends are on the same side of the shank. Press the ends flat with flat-nose pliers.

6 With the cut ends of the wrapping to the inside, bend the shank around the ring mandrel, starting a few sizes smaller than the finished size you desire. Slide it along the mandrel until it's one size larger than the desired size. Take it off the mandrel and remove the tape from both ends.

7 Measure ⅛ inch (0.3 cm) from each end and mark across the wires. Bend the wires 45 degrees at these marks, using flat-nose pliers, to form the mock prongs.

8 Measure and mark the midpoint of the round wire. Feed it through the right-hand opening of one pair of prongs. String the pearl to the wire's midpoint. Position the pearl between the two sets of prongs, then feed the wire through the diagonally opposite prong's bend.

9 Wrap the wire three times around the bends in the shank. Trim any excess wire from inside the ring and press the end flat against the band.

Fiesta Necklace and Earrings

Kate Drew-Wilkinson, Designer

The energetic color
combination of this set
gives the impression
you're wearing a party!

Fiesta Necklace and Earrings

MATERIALS FOR THE NECKLACE

22 red ceramic donut beads, ½ inch (1.3 cm) diameter

27 turquoise round ceramic beads, 8 mm diameter

57 antique copper heishi spacer beads

54 sterling silver round beads, 2.5 mm diameter

20-gauge half-hard silver wire, 6 feet (1.8 m) long

4 silver ball-end head pins, 2 inches (5.1 cm) long

1 pierced silver pendant, 3.5 x 4.5 cm

1 silver S-clasp

FINISHED LENGTH

25½ inches (64.8 cm)

INSTRUCTIONS

1 Set aside 7 donut beads, 11 round ceramic beads, 19 spacers, and 20 sterling silver beads.

2 Cut the wire into 3-inch (7.6 cm) pieces. Using one piece of wire, make a wrapped bead loop link with a sterling silver bead, a spacer, a round ceramic bead, another spacer, and another sterling silver bead on it. Slip a donut on a loop before closing it. Keep the loops large enough to allow the donut free movement.

3 Make another wrapped bead loop link threaded with the same beads as in step 2, slipping the donut from the previous link onto one loop and adding another donut to the loop at the other end. Repeat the process until you've used all the beads except those set aside in step 1. Slip the ends of the S-clasp onto the free loops at the beginning and end of the strand, closing the necklace.

4 Using the beads set aside in step 1, make a bead loop link threaded with the same beads as in step 2. Before closing the second loop, attach it to the sixth donut from the clasp. Repeat, attaching a bead loop link to the next four donuts. Make and attach two more bead loop links on the eighth donut.

5 Make a bead loop link threaded with a sterling silver bead, a spacer, and another sterling silver bead, adding the silver pendant to one loop; attach the other loop to the center link hanging on the eighth donut.

6 Thread a turquoise bead, a spacer, and a sterling silver bead on each ball-end head pin. Attach one each to the fifth and eleventh donuts, and the last two at the ends of the two links on the eighth donut.

MATERIALS FOR THE EARRINGS

20 sterling silver round beads, 2.5 mm diameter

20 copper heishi spacer beads

8 red ceramic donut beads, ½ inch (1.3 cm) diameter

6 turquoise ceramic beads, 8 mm diameter

20-gauge half-hard silver wire, 2 feet (61 cm)

2 ear wires

INSTRUCTIONS

MAKE 2.

1 Cut the wire into 3-inch (7.6 cm) pieces.

2 Make two wrapped bead loop links, threading a sterling silver bead, three spacers, and another sterling silver bead on each; slip an ear wire on one loop end and a donut on the other. Keep one of the loops large enough to allow the donut free movement.

3 Make another wrapped bead loop link with a sterling silver bead, a spacer, and another sterling silver bead threaded on it, attaching one loop to the donut from the previous step and leaving the other loop empty.

4 Make a bead loop link like the ones from step 2 for the necklace. Before closing the loops, attach a donut to one of them, then link the other loop to the empty end of the link from the previous step. Repeat two more times.

Turquoise nuggets and bronze-colored pearls accent this knitted-wire necklace. Its imposing size makes a stunning statement as wearable art.

Opulence Necklace

Susan I. Jones, Designer

MATERIALS

17–20 faceted turquoise pebbles,
¾ inch (1.9 cm) diameter

60 tumbled turquoise nuggets,
½ inch (1.3 cm) diameter

100 turquoise rondelles, 6 mm
diameter

36 round turquoise beads, 8 mm
diameter

30 greenish-gold freshwater pearls,
7 mm diameter

26-gauge gold-tone wire, 30 yards
(27.4 m) long

26-gauge aqua wire, 30 yards
(27.4 m) long

1 gold-tone toggle clasp

TOOLS

Shallow pan or tray

Knitting needles, 10 mm (size 15 U.S.)

FINISHED LENGTH

23¼ inches (59 cm)

INSTRUCTIONS

1 Place all the beads in a pan and mix them. Randomly string all the beads on the separate wires; it's not important to have an equal amount of beads on each, but the first and last 4 inches (10.2 cm) of beads should be only smaller ones, so they will be at the back of the finished piece. Don't cut off the extra wire.

Holding both wire ends tog, make an overhand loop, leaving a tail 10 inches (25.4 cm) long, and CO 2 sts.

Rows 1–3: K2.

Row 4: Inc1, k3, feeding beads from alternating wires as you k in all rows hereafter.

Rows 5–7: K3.

Row 8: Inc1, k4.

K every row until the piece measures 16 inches (40.6 cm) long.

In the next row, dec1 st, k.

K the next 3 rows.

From this point on, stop adding beads as you k. Dec1 st, k.

K 3 rows.

Instead of BO, remove the knitting needles and cut the wires together, leaving a tail 10 inches (25.4 cm) long.

2 Slide off any unused beads. Make an overhand loop in the tails, feed the wire ends through it, and tighten it.

3 Attach one end of the necklace to each piece of the toggle clasp by slipping the tails through its loop, pulling them tight, and twisting the wire five times around the base of the clasp. Trim the wires and hide their raw ends inside a nearby bead.

4 To shape the necklace, poke the large nuggets through the knitting so they all lie on the same side of it. As needed, compress the necklace by hand to give it a smooth curve, making it narrower and longer in places; also gently spread the stitches to make it shorter and wider where necessary. If you notice any bare areas, you can slip a leftover bead onto a short piece of wire and attach it directly to that spot by twisting it around a stitch and burying the raw wire ends into a nearby bead.

Here's a lighthearted, uncomplicated bracelet that's so easy to fashion you can make several in various colors for party favors—or wear them all yourself, gypsy style.

Jellyroll Bracelet

Andrea L. McLester, Designer

MATERIALS

3 disk-shaped resin beads, ⅝ inch (1.6 cm) diameter

3 pieces of 20-gauge anodized wire, each 14 inches (35.6 cm) long, for the jellyroll links

3 pieces of 20-gauge anodized wire, each 2½ inches (6.4 cm) long, for the wrapped bead loop links

2 pieces of 20-gauge anodized wire, each 7 inches (17.8 cm) long, for the clasp

TOOLS

½-inch (1.3 cm) dowel or other mandrel

Round-nose pliers with plastic-coated jaws

FINISHED LENGTH

8¾ inches (22.2 cm)

INSTRUCTIONS

Note: Be aware that the colored coating on anodized and plated wires is soft and can be easily scratched. If you don't have the plastic-coated pliers, wrap your regular ones with plastic tape.

1 To make a jellyroll link, use round-nose pliers to make a 90-degree bend in a 14-inch (35.6 cm) length of wire, 2 inches (5 cm) from one end. Grasp the long end of the wire at the bend so that the pliers' jaws lie parallel to the bent part of the wire (see figure 1). Keeping the wire near the tip of the pliers' jaws, make a spiral until you have 7 inches (17.8 cm) of wire left. The short piece of wire will be standing straight out from the center of the spiral.

2 Using the round-nose pliers, bend the longer section of wire 90 degrees, 2 inches (5.1 cm) from the end, but in the direction opposite that of the bend you made in step 1.

3 Make another spiral at this end of the wire, rolling it in the opposite direction as the first, until the second roll is ½ inch (1.3 cm) from the first.

4 Bend both short ends of the wire, in the same direction, so they lie flat over the spirals. Fold the spirals together, with these short wires to the inside. Coil

FIGURE **1**

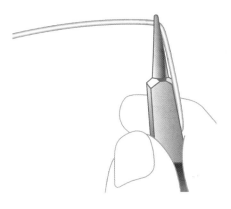

Jellyroll Bracelet

them until they are aligned, one over the other, forming a double-sided "jellyroll" link. See figure 2 for an exploded view of what the element should look like. Make wrapped loops on both ends of the wire.

5 Repeat steps 1 through 4 to make three more jellyroll links.

6 Make a wrapped bead loop link with a resin bead on a 2½-inch (6.4 cm) piece of wire. Before closing each loop, thread a jellyroll link on it. Cut off any excess wire. Repeat at the other end.

7 Connect the two sections with a wrapped bead loop link.

8 To make the eye of the clasp, use a 7-inch (17.8 cm) piece of wire. Make a wrapped loop over the dowel, wrapping the wire twice around it. Thread a resin bead onto the wire, then make a wrapped loop on the other end, slipping a jellyroll link onto the loop before closing it.

9 To make the hook, fold the last piece of wire double, with one end 2 inches (5.1 cm) longer than the other. Do not trim the ends. Use your thumb to fold the bent end of the wire over the dowel. Grasp the folded end of the wire with round-nose pliers and make a loose spiral.

10 Slip the free end of the wire into the loop of the last jellyroll link, then make an extra-long wrapped loop out of the rest of the wire.

FIGURE 2

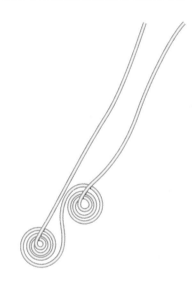

Key to Wire Gauges

The projects in this book were made using wire manufactured in the United States, whose standards for wire diameters differ from those in the British system. AWG is the acronym for American, or Brown & Sharpe, wire gauge sizes and their equivalent rounded metric measurements. SWG is the acronym for the British Standard, or Imperial, system in the UK. Refer to the chart below if you use SWG wire. Only part of the full range of wire gauges that are available from jewelry suppliers is included here.

AWG IN.	AWG MM	GAUGE	SWG IN.	SWG MM
0.204	5.18	4	0.232	5.89
0.182	4.62	5	0.212	5.38
0.162	4.12	6	0.192	4.88
0.144	3.66	7	0.176	4.47
0.129	3.28	8	0.160	4.06
0.114	2.90	9	0.144	3.66
0.102	2.59	10	0.128	3.25
0.091	2.31	11	0.116	2.95
0.081	2.06	12	0.104	2.64
0.072	1.83	13	0.092	2.34
0.064	1.63	14	0.080	2.03
0.057	1.45	15	0.072	1.83
0.051	1.30	16	0.064	1.63
0.045	1.14	17	0.056	1.42
0.040	1.02	18	0.048	1.22
0.036	0.914	19	0.040	1.02
0.032	0.813	20	0.036	0.914
0.029	0.737	21	0.032	0.813
0.025	0.635	22	0.028	0.711
0.023	0.584	23	0.024	0.610
0.020	0.508	24	0.022	0.559
0.018	0.457	25	0.020	0.508
0.016	0.406	26	0.018	0.457

Ruby Wave Bracelet, page 37

About the Designers

Dianne Karg Baron is a Canadian metalsmith who has created jewelry using precious metal wire and gemstones for 10 years. She graduated from Ryerson University with a bachelor of applied arts (interior design) in 1988 and completed the Jewellery Techniques Certificate at George Brown College in Toronto, Ontario, where she now teaches. Dianne has also taught at workshops in Canada and the United States and is a member of the Metal Arts Guild of Canada, the Ontario Crafts Council, and the International Guild of Wire Jewelry Artists. Her work has been featured in craft magazines, including *Lapidary Journal*, and books. She sells her work at galleries and craft shows in Canada, as well as through her website, www.wrapturewirejewellery.on.ca. She lives in Toronto with her husband and kids.

Susan Campanini is crazy about beads. This retired academic began making earrings 15 years ago as gifts for family members, but there just weren't enough earlobes there, so she started selling her creations at local art shows. She loves making one-of-a-kind pieces incorporating all sorts of materials—especially vintage beads and unusual handmade items—and includes wire elements created on a jig by her husband. Her business, Beaded Jewelry by Susan, located in Champaign-Urbana, Illinois, has a huge inventory of more than a thousand unique earrings and hundreds of necklaces … with more to come! She can be reached at campanin@uiuc.edu and sells online through http://www.artisanstreet.com.

Marie Lee Carter began learning her craft in a metalsmithing class at the Fashion Institute of Technology in New York. She used a range of skills that allowed her to work at home without the chemicals and fumes of solder, pickle, and buffing compounds. In each of her unique pieces, Marie aims to tell a short story in precious metal and stone. She can be contacted at marielcarter@verizon.net.

Rachel M. Dow specializes in fabricated sterling silver, metal clay, and found object jewelry. She has a BA in photography and an MA in art education from California State University of Northridge. When she's not banging on metal, she runs around with her three-year-old son and works with fiber. Rachel's work is shown in selected galleries and studios. She lives in Rolla, Missouri, and maintains a website at www.rmddesigns.com.

Kate Drew-Wilkinson was born and raised in England and began her professional life as an actress. She was always fascinated by the history and magic of beads, however, and during her travels in many countries, she studied their use in jewelry. By 1990 Kate had discovered the joy of lampworking. She has written two books on bead jewelry, 48 articles for *Lapidary Journal*, and she also makes instructional films. Kate teaches bead jewelry design and lampworked bead making in Europe.

Connie Fox teaches wire jewelry and cold connections. She and her husband, Jim, operate Jatayu, an Internet wire jewelry business. A nasty allergy to flowers led Connie to explore the wondrous world of wire jewelry; ask her sometime and she'll tell you all about it. She may be contacted through her website, www.conniefox.com.

Ellen Gerritse taught fine art in Europe for a long time but now has the opportunity to travel the world extensively. After a recent move to the United States, she received an MFA in jewelry from the Glassell School of Art in Houston, Texas. The greatest influences on her work have come from traveling in Asia. Being constantly on the move, with a limited knowledge of local suppliers, she finds herself drawn to create objects from simple, accessible materials and the few tools close at hand. She finds this way of working challenging to her way of thinking.

Joanna Gollberg is a studio artist working in Asheville, North Carolina. She graduated from the Fashion Institute of Technology with a degree in jewelry design, and exhibits her work at craft fairs and galleries throughout the United States. Joanna has designed projects for *Fabulous Jewelry from Found Objects* (Lark Books, 2005), and she is the author of two books, *Making Metal Jewelry* (Lark Books, 2003) and *Creative Metal Crafts* (Lark Books, 2004). Joanna has also taught workshops at John C. Campbell Folk School and the Penland School of Crafts.

Diane Guelzow is a wife, mom, special education teacher, empty-nester, art educator, and a lady who likes to keep busy. Making jewelry serves as therapy in the fast-paced world in which she lives because it slows her down and allows her to mellow out and listen to what her soul wants her to express. For Diane, working with sterling silver wire and beads is like working with little treasures collected throughout her life, or akin to keeping a journal; she reveals her "life's diary" through her jewelry. And, boy, there's a lot to tell! She can be reached at artandmind@yahoo.com.

Michaelanne Hall is a self-taught artist living in Asheville, North Carolina. She sells her jewelry in a gallery there. Her e-mail address is MichaelanneOrig@aol.com.

syndee holt is a polymer clay designer and professional photographer, as well as a band mom and a kendo mom. She writes for many national and international magazines and teaches throughout the world. Her website is http://synspage.com.

Susan I. Jones creates over-the-top bead and fiber art in her studio, and there is little that escapes her zeal to embellish. She has a firm belief that chocolate should be on every materials list. Susan lives with her husband, Skip, and two cats in artistic chaos in Chandler, Arizona. Her e-mail address is susanijones@hotmail.com.

Ronda Kivett is a self-taught mixed-media artist who lives in Prescott Valley, Arizona. Her creativity thrives on experimenting with many different materials, but her preferred medium has always been beads. Ronda's work has appeared in exhibitions and galleries across the United States, as well as in books and magazines. Visit her website at www.kivett-studio.com.

Mami Laher is a jewelry designer and artist who loves, more than anything, searching for originality and uniqueness in creative expression. She prides herself on making bead and wire jewelry with no jig, only basic tools. She enjoys painting with watercolors and has an affinity for flowers, abstract as well as real. She can also often be found ice-skating. Mami originally hails from Japan but now resides in Los Angeles. View a sampling of her jewelry, glass beads, and paintings on her website at www.mamibeads.com.

Elizabeth Larsen works as a biologist for Snohomish County in Washington but started beading as a hobby four years ago to challenge her creative side. She particularly enjoys working with sterling silver wire and semiprecious stones. She lives in Snohomish with her husband, Mitch, her stepson, Nico, and their three dogs, Misha, Rocky, and Cordelia. Her e-mail address is elarsen2003@yahoo.com.

Andrea L. McLester has had the pleasure, as a theatrical designer and costumer, of creating jewelry for some of the world's legendary ballerinas and opera singers. She currently resides in Rockport, Texas, where she is represented by The Gallery of Rockport.

Nathalie Mornu definitely doesn't hold with the theory that less is more where shiny things are concerned. She has designed projects for other Lark books, including *Decorating Your First Apartment* (2002), *Hip Handbags* (2005), *Exquisite Embellishments for Your Clothes* (2006), and *Creative Stitching on Paper* (2006).

Eni Oken's jewelry embraces an eclectic mix of techniques and precious materials. Fantasy art, sculpture, architecture, and lace-making techniques all come together in her intricate and ornamental designs. Originally from Brazil, Eni now lives in Los Angeles, where she explores new techniques and creates. She also writes and teaches about art and jewelry making. You can see more of Eni's work and her lessons at www.enioken.com.

Chris Orcutt has worked as a jeweler since 1985, fabricating one-of-a-kind jewelry by hand. She loves her current job as a goldsmith, jewelry designer, and salesperson at the Metal Waterfall Gallery and Christine Ann Jewelry in downtown Leavenworth, Washington. Christine also sells her unique pieces through an online auction, which can be accessed at www.christineannjewelry.com.

Carolyn Skei is a mixed-media artist who has many years of experience with polymer clay jewelry making, fiber arts, papermaking, bookbinding, and experimental photography. An admitted "workshop junkie," she loves both to teach and to learn new techniques. In 2000 Carolyn relocated from California to her native Texas. She has taught for the Craft Guild of Dallas, the Brazosport Center for the Arts and Sciences, and the North Texas Polymer Clay Guild. A certified Texas Master Gardener, she draws much of her inspiration from the ecosystem in her own backyard. She may be reached at ctexasskei@comcast.net.

Marinda Stewart is a designer, writer, and teacher who resides in Santa Maria, California. Her accomplishments include a line of patterns for clothing and accessories, many magazine and book contributions, television appearances, national ads, and several embellishment books. Her work has appeared in museum and gallery exhibitions and is in the collections of several corporations and celebrities. She currently works with corporate clients, designing and consulting on end uses for their products. Her website is at www.marindastewart.com.

Hanni Yothers grew up on Lake Huron in Michigan's beautiful Upper Peninsula, where huge old trees, wildlife, and incredible views surrounded her childhood home and instilled in her a love of all things natural. When she discovered stones and metal and realized that these pieces of the earth could be made into beautiful jewelry, her career path was set. She has designed, created, and sold her jewelry worldwide for more than 12 years, and lives with her husband, five golden retrievers, two red-tail hawks, and assorted chickens. View her jewelry on the Internet at www.heyjewelry.com.

Acknowledgments

This book wouldn't have seen the light of day without the talented designers who shared their fabulous work and creative energy with us. They were a pleasure to work with, and we're grateful for their great ideas and flexibility.

We're indebted to Chevron Trading Post & Bead Company, for graciously lending us many of the lovely beads and tools that illustrate the Basics section of this book. Stop by their well-stocked store if you're ever in Asheville, North Carolina, or visit their website at www.chevronbeads.com.

We also appreciate the loan of additional tools from our colleague Terry Taylor.

Thank you to Orrin Lundgren for his precise illustrations that shine as a guiding beacon.

Our deepest thanks go to Stewart O'Shields for producing the gorgeous photographs that grace these pages, and to Stacey Budge for styling an elegant book.

Nathalie Mornu and Suzanne J. E. Tourtillott

Wandering Gypsy Bracelet,
page 35

Index

Beaded Dragonfly Brooch,
page 78